Successfully Navigating
the Mortgage Maze

Successfully Navigating the Mortgage Maze

Save Thousands on Your Loan
Avoid Dishonest Lenders and Brokers
Find the Lowest Rates and Fees
Understand Your Loan Documents

Alan L. Jablonski, Esq.
Consumer Rights Attorney

iUniverse, Inc.
New York Bloomington Shanghai

Successfully Navigating the Mortgage Maze
Save Thousands on Your Loan Avoid Dishonest Lenders and Brokers Find
the Lowest Rates and Fees Understand Your Loan Documents

Copyright © 2008 by Alan L. Jablonski

iUniverse books may be ordered through booksellers or by contacting:

iUniverse
1663 Liberty Drive
Bloomington, IN 47403
www.iuniverse.com
1-800-Authors (1-800-288-4677)

Because of the dynamic nature of the Internet, any Web addresses
or links contained in this book may have changed
since publication and may no longer be valid.

The views expressed in this work are solely those of the author and do
not necessarily reflect the views of the publisher, and the publisher hereby
disclaims any responsibility for them.

ISBN: 978-0-595-52145-6 (pbk)
ISBN: 978-0-595-62210-8 (ebk)

Printed in the United States of America

"Love all, trust few."

William Shakespeare

Contents

About the Author... xi

Acknowledgements xiii

Introduction...xv

Chapter 1

The Mortgage Industry...1
    Brief History of the Mortgage Industry...................................1
    Laws Offer Little Protection 3
    Lender vs. Brokers: What's the Difference?..............................7
    Preying on Your Emotions 9
    Shopping for Rates..9
    Mortgage Advertising: The Numbers can be Misleading 11
    Can Anyone be Trusted? 13

Chapter 2

The Mortgage Language: Why It's So Important 17

Chapter 3

The Process & Players: Who Does What? 26

Chapter 4

Fees: Who Gets What 34
    Up-front Fees 35
    Origination Fees 35
    Escrow Fees 37
    Title fees 38
    Non-fixed Fees 39
    Property Taxes & Homeowner's Insurance 41

Chapter 5

The Hidden Cost of Your Loan 42
    Yield Spread Premium or Rebate...42

Wholesale Rate Sheet 43

Checking Daily Interest Rates 44

Finding Out How Much Your Loan is Costing You 47

Chapter 6

Qualifying for Your Loan; How Your Rates are Determined 49

The Mortgage Bond Market..49

Your Credit (FICO Scores & Credit History) 50

Debt to Income Ratio (DTI) 52

Types of Loans (Fixed, Adjustable and Others) 53

Fixed Loans 54

Adjustable Rate Mortgages (ARMs) 55

Option ARM (Pick a Pay) Loan 56

Federal Housing Administration (FHA) Loans 59

Stated Income Loans 60

Loan to Value (LTV)/Combined Loan of Value (CLTV) 61

Purchase/Refinance/Cash-Out Refinance................................63

Prepayment Penalty 64

Chapter 7

Understanding Your Loan Documents 67

Good Faith Estimate (GFE) 68

Loan Totals & Monthly Payment 74

Promissory Note 75

Truth in Lending Statement 77

Settlement Statement (HUD-1)..82

Chapter 8

Finding an Honest Broker or Lender and Working with Them 88

Referral from Family or Friends 88

Comparing Rates 89

Interviewing Your Loan Officer 89

Commitments to Request 92

Working with Your Loan Officer...94
If Your Fees or Rate Has Changed..95
Conclusion 96

About the Author...

First time author, Alan Jablonski, is one of Southern California's most prominent consumer rights attorneys and a licensed California mortgage broker. He is a sought-after presenter on mortgage and credit issues for companies in both the public and private sectors.

Alan has been a practicing attorney in the State of California for the past eight years, four of which were spent representing foster children in the Los Angeles County foster care system, the nations largest.

Alan opened his private practice in 2004, specializing in credit-related matters and their affect on home borrowers. He has earned a stellar reputation for identifying the predatory lending practices of mortgage companies and protecting homeowners from high-cost and high-interest rate loans.

For the past three years Alan has been an arbitrator for the Better Business Bureau of Southern California. He also sat on the Board of Directors for the California Family Life Center, a charity that aids foster children and juveniles under court supervision, and The First Step House of Orange County, which provides services for indigent alcoholics focused on turning their lives around.

Acknowledgements

I would like to acknowledge the mentorship of Doug O'Keefe, a thirty-three-year veteran of the mortgage industry, who contributed to my knowledge of the mortgage industry with an emphasis on fair dealing with clients. Also, Superior Court Judge William Monroe for instilling a sense of compassion for the clients I serve.

I appreciate the assistance of Calyx Software for granting permission to use their form templates, so the readers of this guide can see the documents that many lenders and brokers use in the industry.

I would like to thank my friends from Thursday night, Cam, Paul, Wyatt, Doug, Marcus and Chip for being there for me during my recovery from surgery. They reminded me that no matter our present circumstances we can help those around us to achieve a quiet mind and a peaceful heart.

Most importantly, Alan would like to thank Teri, Mary, Richard and Kevin Jablonski, without whose love and support this guide would not have been possible.

Introduction

This guide is dedicated to homeowners and prospective homeowners whose only wish is to be dealt with honestly and fairly by the mortgage company they choose to finance their loan.

In an industry that has more than its fair share of unscrupulous lenders and brokers, this guide will assist you in navigating the loan process, separating hype from reality, and lowering the stress that occurs when financing your home. By understanding what questions to ask, along with important facts about your credit, income qualifications and how the mortgage industry operates you will be in the driver's seat during the loan process.

Most borrowers spend more time investigating which appliance or DVD player to buy than whom to work with while taking on the largest debt they will incur in their life, their mortgage. The loan process need not be filled with confusion and apprehension. This guide will show you how to avoid the dishonest loan officers and understand the most important documents involved with your loan.

A few years ago my wife and I began the process of purchasing our first home. We were promised a low rate, low monthly payments and less than $6,000 in fees. We trusted the mortgage broker because she was recommended by our realtor. By the time the signing took place, our monthly payments had increased by $240 and our loan costs exceeded $11,000. The broker knew I was a practicing attorney, but that did not stop her from hiding the details of our loan. As the notary prepared for our signing, I asked my wife if she was willing to lose our home and sadly she agreed. I fired our mortgage broker on the spot and sent the notary packing.

My wife was devastated and I was in total disbelief. Since the day we signed the purchase agreement, this home had become ours. The broker knew the strong emotional attachment we had formed towards this home; in fact she counted on it, believing we would sign the loan regardless of the changes. Surveys show that over 80% of borrowers will sign the documents, even if the loan was not what they were promised.

We either had to find another lender or give up the home. This brings me to an important point; we found another broker and she kept all of her commitments, saving our home. There are honest loan officers out there; the difficulty is finding them.

I believe this guide will help you avoid the ordeal my wife and I experienced, by finding a broker or lender that will give you a good rate and low costs without misleading you during the process. This guide contains 30 Rules that all borrowers should follow and a step-by-step interviewing process that will weed out the dishonest loan officers.

Chapter 1

The Mortgage Industry

Brief History of the Mortgage Industry

The mortgage industry is filled with lenders and brokers looking to make a fast buck at your expense. Over the last decade while loan officers were filling their bank accounts with your money, they demonstrated a total disregard for the borrower's finances. This was not necessary and could have been avoided by proper preparation on the part of the borrower. While there are many legitimate and trust worthy loan officers, finding them is a daunting task. With the help of this guide, you will learn how to find and interview a loan officer to determine whether they have your interests at heart or that of their bank account.

Over the past decade everyone had a loan officer in the family, friend or acquaintance that could help them with their mortgage. You could throw a stone out the window and hit one. In 2005, there were over 500,000 loan officers in the United States. In 2008, that number had dropped to 165,000. The industry had teenagers and individuals with criminal records handling your most private financial information, steering borrowers to loans that were financial disasters. In the last year, many who were in the industry for the quick cash have left for greener pastures or prison. This is no time to let down your guard, however, because some of the worst offenders are still out there making promises they do not intend to keep. It will cost you thousands in unnecessary interest payments and fees if you are not prepared.

> "Foreclosure projections for 2008-2009 are estimated to reach 2,258,457, many of which, will be caused by Adjustable Rate Mortgages (ARMs) entering their adjustable period."

The mortgage industry underwent great changes with the entry of thousands of lenders and brokers in the 1990s, who served the financial needs of borrowers across the nation. Individuals with less than stellar credit could reach the goal of homeownership-the same buyers who a few years earlier found homeownership totally out reach. The competition was fierce and the huge fees that were charged in the early 1980s have lowered dramatically. In the early 1980s lenders would require 10 to 20 Points (10%-20% of your loan) in fees for providing a borrower with a mortgage loan. Gladly, those days are long gone and the average "A" paper loan will cost 1.5 Points (1 1/2%) if you are working with a reputable broker or lender.

Sub-prime borrowers have had to pay higher interest rates historically for shorter fixed periods. Many sub-prime borrowers were talked into paying 4 or 5 Points (4-5% of their mortgage) to fund their loan and believed the lender was doing them a favor. The truth is that it's no more difficult to process a sub-prime loan than an "A" paper loan, if the sub-prime borrower qualifies for a particular product. There should be no difference in fees for producing their loan.

> "Lack of transparency and the complexity of the loans in the sub-prime market make it all but impossible for consumers to know if they are being overcharged."
>
> Center for Responsible Lending
> April 8, 2008

Many "A" paper loans are purchased by Fannie Mae and Freddie Mac. These Government Sponsored Enterprises (GSEs) were created by the federal government to provide greater access to money that lenders needed to meet the demands of an ever-increasing home purchase market. If a loan meets their guidelines, the loan will be bought or insured by Fannie Mae or Freddie Mac, removing the risk from the lender. Sub-prime loans are financed by private investors and this is the reason rates are considerably higher for these borrowers. Many "A" paper borrowers are steered to more expensive sub-prime loans, even though they qualify for prime rates, because lenders and brokers make more money on sub-prime products.

> "Predatory lending costs Americans an estimated $9.1 billion each year."
>
> Center for Responsible Lending
>
> February 23, 2006

Later in this guide, I will assist you with finding those lenders and brokers that will not increase their net worth at your expense. Many readers will want to jump to Chapter 8 and begin the interviewing process. But, it is critical that you understand the language of the industry, what affects your rates and the loan documents that provide you with all the information you need to protect yourself. I urge you to read the entire guide, it will give you a well-rounded education to avoid the traps that brokers and lenders set for you at the beginning of the loan process. Currently, the only defense a borrower has is to become as well-informed as possible because there are no laws that will ultimately protect them during the loan process.

Laws Offer Little Protection

Federal laws have been enacted in a poor attempt to stop predatory leading practices, but as always, many in the industry have learned how to use these laws to their advantage. The "Truth in Lending Act" was passed in 1968, part of the Consumer Protection Act, as politicians made a half-hearted attempt to protect the public. The Act required certain disclosures, such as the APR (Annual Percentage Rate) and finance charges associated with home loans. It required that advertisements contain certain disclosures to avoid misleading the consumer. Politicians left enough loopholes so that lending institutions and their loan officers could continue misleading borrowers. It would be rather simple to pass laws that require full disclosure, but the lobbying interests of these institutions are too large and make huge contributions on both sides of the political isle. Borrowers are left to their own devices, but if the average homeowner cannot understand the traps set during the initial conversations, then the documents will surely overwhelm them when it comes time for signing.

The Real Estate Settlement Procedures Act (RESPA) was enacted in 1974 to remove the kickbacks many in the industry received and to help consumers become better loan shoppers. On the Department of Housing's website, the Department proudly displays RESPA's requirement that borrowers receive a Good Faith Estimate (GFE) to review the costs of their loan. The very next statement advises borrowers that the GFE is only an estimate and the terms can change. We have all seen what has happened in the housing and mortgage markets over the past two years. Homeowners across the nation are struggling to make the mortgage payments on loans that they were deceived into accepting. The crash of the housing market has demonstrated how ineffectual current laws are in protecting unwary borrowers.

Many states have taken the lead in protecting consumers from predatory and dishonest lenders. In a recent study by the Center for Responsible Lending, four states; New Mexico, Massachusetts, North Carolina and West Virginia have the strongest laws protecting consumers at this time. It is important to point out that although tougher laws will help the consumer, it will always fall to the consumer to protect themselves from unscrupulous lenders and brokers.

Both State and Federal enforcement agencies along with the legal community have a great deal of difficulty enforcing the predatory lending laws at this time. The Department of Housing and Urban Development has identified some types of "Predatory Lending" such as approving a loan without considering the borrower's ability to repay the loan. None of the current federal laws provide a clear definition so they are open to a wide array of interpretations. What may be predatory in one loan scenario may not be in another. This leaves government agencies and attorneys to interpret each instance differently, as if using the old definition of pornography, "I don't know how to define it, but I know it when I see it."

If RESPA or the Truth-in-Leading Act is violated, borrowers may have legal recourse if it can be proven that the lender engaged in predatory lending or deceptive trade practices. Unless new proposals leave no room for deception, though, the mortgage industry's unscrupulous lenders and brokers will find a way to circumvent any new disclosure laws and consumers will be left swimming in the same shark-infested waters they swim in today. New disclosure proposals will have to make their way through Congress and past the industry's lobbyists, so they will likely be watered down.

> According to past Senate testimony, "under current disclosure laws, 83% of borrowers get stuck with higher closing costs and rates than originally promised."

Individuals within our government who have been given oversight and enforcement powers have not taken appropriate action to protect consumers from the predators within the mortgage industry. Alan Greenspan, the former Chairman of the Federal Reserve, was advising borrowers to accept adjustable-rate mortgages at a time when these loans were the worst possible option for homeowners. These adjustable mortgages assisted lenders and investors with their bottom line. Greenspan was too busy protecting the financial markets at the expense of homeowners. In 2007, $200 Billion in loans turned adjustable. In 2008, an estimated $1 Trillion in loans will turn adjustable. There is no indication there will be any easing of the foreclosure rate caused by these adjustable rate mortgages any time soon.

Ameriquest, one of the country's largest lenders made $1.3 Billion in 2005, was sued by 49 states for unfair and deceptive trade practices. Investors soon pulled out and Ameriquest filed for bankruptcy. What did the CEO of Ameriquest, Roland Arnall, receive beyond multiple mansions and over a billion dollars in assets? He was appointed the United States Ambassador to the Netherlands. I hope he didn't try to start a mortgage company in their country; it would not have helped United States-Netherlands relations.

The mortgage industry and investment community are paying the price for playing it fast and loose with borrowers, as the recent bailout of Bear Sterns has demonstrated. Most sub-prime lenders have filed for bankruptcy and the lending requirements for all other mortgage loans have been tightened over the last year. The real victims of the financial crisis are current homeowners who have seen their property values plummet through no fault of their own.

The "economic stimulus package" passed in early 2008 purported to help distressed homeowners avoid foreclosure. The true beneficiaries of this package were the lending and investment communities. The package provided very little help, if any, to homeowners caught in high interest rate loans. Do our politicians really care about the average homeowner? It is difficult to say, but it is interesting to note that the bankruptcy laws were changed in 2005 to protect creditors, not the consumers. Credit industry insiders saw the trouble coming years ago and through their lobbyists had the federal government make it more difficult to file for Chapter 7 or 13 bankruptcy protection.

Recently, the Department of Housing and Urban Development released a "proposed mortgage relief package" to press for changes in disclosure laws among other proposals, so borrowers would understand the type of loan they are receiving and the fees that accompany them. The proposals state that all Yield Spread Premiums (fees lenders and brokers receive for raising your interest rate) should be disclosed to the borrower in plain language. Just how these proposals will be enacted is difficult to foresee, since the lending industry's lobbyists are forever on guard against any changes in the current disclosure laws.

> "But I do believe that, in the long run, markets are better than regulators at allocating credit."
>
> Ben Bernanke
> Chairman, Federal Reserve
> May 17, 2007

One lender after another has fallen into financial distress and they all have the same answer: "It's not our fault." There is a total lack of responsibility on the part of lenders and investors who helped create the mess we are now in. We would not be experiencing the meltdown in the housing and mortgage industry that we see today with strengthened disclosure requirements. According to comments by Ben Bernanke, Chairman of the Federal Reserve, the lending industry will be better at regulating their lending practices without further government oversight.

Rule #1

"Don't rely on new laws to protect your interests; you must protect yourself."

Lender vs. Brokers: What's the Difference?

Borrowers can choose to work with a direct lender or broker to assist them with their mortgage financing. Direct lenders have their own money to loan, while brokers act as intermediaries who search among many different lenders for the best possible loan for their borrowers. There are advantages and disadvantages when you choose to work with either one. Whether you choose a lender or broker, there are many considerations that must be thoroughly explored to find the best interest rate and the lowest costs for you.

Banks and other lending institutions that act as direct lenders usually have strict guidelines that their loan officers must follow. This doesn't mean they are giving you a good loan. These direct lenders have specific products that cater to a particular borrower. It is possible to get a very good rate from a direct lender, but you can not always be sure it is the best available in the market on any given day. No one lender serves all the market niches (every borrower's situation is different), but if you have the time to rate shop with a few different lenders this could be a good starting point for you. Rate shopping can also be a complete waste of time, if you do not know the current interest rates before calling the lenders.

Brokers, on the other hand, are usually approved with multiple lenders and they do the shopping for you. Recent market surveys show brokers handle over 60% of all loans originated in the United States. Many borrowers are under the misconception that they will have to pay more for their loan because a middleman is involved. This is far from the truth, since brokers receive wholesale or discounted rates from lenders to draw the brokers to their institution. Generally, brokers will be offered rates that are .25% to .5% below the rate that lenders offer to the public. It is more likely that a broker will attempt to fit you into a loan that you do not qualify for and you run the risk of being rejected by the lender's underwriter after you have started the loan process. Brokers have a tendency to throw mud against the wall and hope something sticks.

A professional broker can save you time and money by searching multiple lenders to see who has the best rates on any given day. That doesn't mean they are going to shop for you, but most do make the effort to find the lowest rates. By using a broker, you have a greater ability to negotiate on their fees. Most lenders do not give their loan officers this authority, and getting an interest rate as close to the par rate (the lowest rate available) with low fees is the goal.

> "In the first four years of a mortgage, a typical sub-prime borrower, who has used a broker, paid $5,222 more than if going to a direct lender."
>
> Center for Responsible Lending
>
> April 8, 2008

There are broker correspondents, who have credit lines extended to them by banks allowing them to act as a mortgage banker, rather than a broker. Also, there are brokers that have warehouse lines; without getting into detail, they act as a lender by grouping all the loans funded by a particular lender and selling them in large portfolio of loans.

Lenders, broker correspondents and brokers with warehouse lines do not have to disclose that they are raising your rate to make more money on your loan. An independent broker gives you the best opportunity to see all the fees that you are paying for your loan when the time comes for signing. They are required to disclose the Yield Spread Premium, the fee for raising your interest rate above the par rate, on the Settlement Statement (HUD-1). Additionally, by using a broker in your area, you have a better chance at lower fees because the broker will benefit from referrals if their clients have a good experience. How to find an honest broker or lender will be explained in Chapter 8.

Rule #2

"Knowledge is the key; a well informed borrower can control the loan process and the fees."

Preying on Your Emotions

Most loan officers have no idea what the best interests of their clients are; and worse many in the industry see nothing but a target, ready to wring as much money out of you as they possibly can. Increases to the agreed-upon interest rate and fees at the time of your signing can leave you with the feeling that you were betrayed and powerless to do anything about it.

Purchasing a home is a very emotional experience, whether you are a first-time home buyer or it's your retirement home. This is no less true for a refinance. In your mind the home is exactly what you have been looking for and is already yours. Loan officers will take advantage of this emotional tie to a home, believing that if they increase the rate or fees later in the process, you will sign the documents regardless of these changes. They are correct-according to past surveys, most buyers will sign the loan documents even if they see costly changes, because they don't want to start the process again.

Rule #3

"Never fall in love with a piece of property."

There were brokers and lenders that broke their loan officers into teams with names such as the "bait and switchers" and "prepay kings" that denoted their intent to take advantage of their clients. I worked with borrowers after they came into my office in tears, on the verge of losing their homes, desperately trying to find a way out of the adjustable loan that an unscrupulous lender or broker had given them without their knowledge. Many of the worst offenders are still out there, but there are ways to reduce your exposure to these bloodsuckers.

Shopping for Rates

The mortgage industry did not get its poor reputation because loan officers are looking out for your interests. Most will do or say anything to fund a loan for you. Promises of great interest rates and low fees are found across the board even if they have no basis in reality. Loan officers know that if they don't get you to commit to them in the first conversation, they have probably lost the loan. All loan officers want to be the last person you speak with regarding your mortgage needs.

Much of the problem lies with the industry's disreputable lenders and brokers, but borrowers play a significant role in creating their own difficulties. When rate shopping, a borrower will more likely use a loan officer who paints a rosy picture and underestimates the rate and costs of the loan. The borrower finds out weeks into the loan process that the numbers were a sham.

Rule #4

"The goal of the loan officer is to get you started in the process; using any means necessary to get your credit information, most importantly, your Social Security number."

Additionally, many borrowers during the initial conversation with the lender or broker will inflate their credit scores, income and savings. All of which will directly affect the loan you qualify for and the fees associated with the loan. Many hours have been wasted by loan officers who take the word of borrowers without any confirmation of the numbers they are receiving, only to find that none of the information was accurate. Small changes in income, savings or the property value can have a great impact on qualifying for a loan. Loan officers get paid for funded loans, not for speaking with borrowers about hypothetical scenarios. Many loan officers will not waste their time with someone who doesn't give them the ability to check their credit scores at the outset. Who can blame them? The time spent with someone who has no idea what their real credit scores are could have been time spent with a real prospect for a loan. Professionals understand that a brief discussion with a borrower without demanding their Social Security number is part of our business. Don't give anyone your Social Security number if they won't answer your questions first.

Checking your credit scores is not just done to see what type of loan you are qualified for. It is deeply psychological. Once you have released your financial information, the odds that you will continue shopping for a good loan greatly decrease. Most borrowers will not want to give their Social Security number to multiple lenders, even if red flags pop up later in the conversation warning you that this person is not to be trusted.

Mortgage Advertising: The Numbers can be Misleading

I have spent countless hours searching advertisements that demonstrate integrity on the part of lenders and brokers. There has never been full disclosure in any of these marketing campaigns. The Truth in Lending Act has been a complete failure with regards to advertising integrity within the mortgage industry.

Initial warnings of a dishonest lender or broker:

1. They state that no one can give you the loan they are offering.

2. They say, you have to commit immediately, or they can't do the loan.

3. They do so many loans they can lower their interest rates.

4. They require a deposit to begin the loan process.

5. They won't talk to you without getting your Social Security number.

6. They say they have lower rates than anyone else.

7. They tell you, don't trust anyone else, but them.

8. They won't answer your questions, but talk about their personal life.

9. They ask questions like "Do you want to pay your loan off faster?"

One example of these ads is "Take money out of your home and lower your payment." Does this really make any sense in light of increasing the amount you owe? Do you really think your payment can go down for the same type of loan? If you move to an "Interest Only" payment or lower your rate significantly it is possible. Remember, you must compare apples to apples, and loan officers can be great deceivers.

This is my favorite; "You come in with a $300,000 loan and you leave with a $300,000 loan; we're making plenty of money off the interest." These companies raise your rate, making their money in rebates (fees for raising the interest rate above the par rate) without charging you for the loan up-front.

> "Avoid working with any lender or broker who called you offering a great rate and low cost loan. Companies that have not built good relationships with their past clients (because they took them for everything they could) are the only entities that use telemarketing to find new loan prospects."

Advertisements can create the illusion that a particular lender or broker can give you an extremely low rate as compared to their competitors. What the advertisement doesn't tell you is that to receive their rate you must pay large fees (pre-paid interest) to buy down the interest rate.

In addition, the advertisement doesn't tell you that you must pay title and escrow fees because they are not lender fees. Most borrowers want to know the total costs of their loan, not just a small part of the fees. In addition, this lender or broker isn't telling you that your interest rate is well above the par rate (lowest wholesale rate available) because no one does loans for free and they will make their money by raising your rate and avoiding origination fees.

Interest Rate:	6%	Interest Rate:	5.75%
APR:	6.125%	APR:	5.99%

Looking at the example above, most consumers would believe the 5.75% interest rate is a better deal because the APR is lower than the actual interest rate of the first example. The truth is that the 5.75% interest rate will cost you $10,200 and the 6% interest rate will cost you $5,300. That's a $4,900 difference. But you may think well at least I'm getting a lower interest rate, which is true, but on a $400,000 loan, the difference in the monthly payment is $64/month. It will take 77 months (6.4 years) to break even on the loan. The lending industry has spent $188 million through their Washington D.C. lobbyists to ensure consumers don't understand the real costs of their loan.

Rule #5

"Advertisements are designed to get you to call; don't believe any of the numbers."

Can Anyone be Trusted?

Beyond the lenders and brokers there are other companies that will play a significant role in your purchase or refinance. Realtors, title and escrow companies, appraisers and property inspectors have a role in completing your loan. Can these companies be trusted to look out for your financial interests?

Realtors, as with the lending industry, have their fair share of dishonest practitioners. There are many hard-working realtors who are dedicated to helping their clients find a home they love at a price they can afford. As with loan officers, home buyers should interview at least three to five realtors to find one that they are comfortable working with. Discovering who will deal with you in a fair and consistent manner is outside the scope of this guide, but there are many how-to books to help you find and work with an honest realtor.

Title and escrow companies serve a necessary role in the processing of your loan. Lenders and brokers have formed relationships with the title and escrow officers so that your loan will be completed in a timely manner. There are companies that have title and escrow services under one roof and there are those that focus only on title or escrow. I work with a company that offers both services and have never been surprised with added fees or changes to their stated fees during the loan process. Brokers and lenders know exactly what the fees will be at the beginning of the process.

Title companies investigate the history of a property's ownership, tax liens and easements attached to a property. It is their job to make sure that no one else has a claim on your home that would create what is called a "cloud on title" in legal terminology. These clouds may be past fraudulent transfers, unpaid property taxes or some right of access to the land that has been granted. Borrowers are required to purchase a title policy because the lender's interest in the property could be challenged at a later date. The policy will protect the lender and you if someone claims a right to the property after the closing of your loan. The title company will record your deed with the County, sadly to let the County assessors' office know who has to pay the taxes in the coming years.

Many consumer rights organizations believe that title companies overcharge for their services. This belief is based on the small percentage of claims that are made under these policies. The title industry argues that the cost is due to keeping their records up to date. At this time, title fees are not negotiable. If your property is located in California, you can visit www.titlewizard.com to compare rates by various title companies. When purchasing a home, the seller can choose the escrow company, but the buyer retains the right to choose the title company. Since the seller's interest in the property ends at closing, it is the buyer who must be happy with the title policy that was purchased. Many realtors, lenders and brokers ignore this law and don't tell you about it.

Escrow companies have a fiduciary duty to all parties in a transaction. Basically, they have to make sure that all the documents are in order and the escrow instructions given by the lender are followed. Your escrow agent will open up escrow at the beginning of the purchase or refinance. Escrow agents ensure that all the money is transferred to the proper parties at the closing of your loan. Your escrow officer is responsible for the signing of your documents. The signing may be conducted by the escrow agent or a mobile notary can visit you at your home.

When purchasing a home, a property inspector must be employed to inspect all the nooks and crannies of your home, looking for damage (water drainage problems, termites, etc.). Many realtors have inspectors that they regularly refer their clients to for the inspection. Find an independent home inspector to conduct the inspection. Think about it for a moment-if the realtor's home inspector continually points out every flaw in a property, would they continue to receive the referrals?

Rule #6

"Don't hire a property inspector that your realtor has referred you to when purchasing a property."

Be present for the inspection and make sure he is crawling underneath the home, going up on the roof and checking the wood for termite damage, not just walking around conducting a poor inspection. Ask questions about the problems that he observes and if problems are present use these to lower the asking price of the property. Minor problems will not be reported by the appraiser, but even small problems can cost you thousands to repair. By having a thorough inspection you can address any problems in your negotiations with the seller.

Another professional that is critical to your purchase or refinance is the appraiser. Appraisers are licensed by the state in which they conduct their appraisals and must undergo significant training and testing to ensure they know how to value your home. Beyond the state licensing, appraisers must be authorized by the lender to value properties. Most lenders will allow any licensed appraiser to conduct the appraisal, but many lenders have a list of appraisers who are no longer authorized to perform their appraisals due to their history of overvaluing homes to make sure the loans were completed.

Demands by realtors and brokers to reach the value needed for a particular home is a challenge faced by all appraisers. It is illegal for a lender or broker to request a value to meet the loan requirements prior to the appraisal taking place. This law was instituted to protect the public from dishonest realtors and brokers who, for the most, are not interested in whether you are paying too much for your home, but prefer just to get the deal done so they can get paid.

When appraisals are submitted to lenders, the appraisal is the property of your lender or broker although you paid for it. This doesn't make any sense and a law needs to be enacted to allow the appraiser to change the broker's name if you decide to move to a different company after the appraisal has been completed. You can attempt to protect yourself if you change to a new lender or broker by getting a commitment in writing that the company will allow the appraisal to be transferred to a new lender or broker in the event you choose to work with a new company in the coming weeks.

Not being able to confirm a property's value creates a problem for the borrower. If your loan does not reach the required value to make the loan possible, you just spent money for an appraisal ($350 and up) that accomplished nothing. Most brokers and lenders have relationships with appraisers such that they can ask where they think the value will fall prior to the appraisal. There is no guarantee the home's value will support the loan, but dishonest lenders and brokers will tell you it will, even if the value is highly questionable.

I had a client who had fallen in love with a condo and wanted no other property but that particular condo. The sale price of the condo was significantly over-priced. I contacted my appraiser and ask for an estimate on the condo's value and he confirmed that the price was not in line with its real value. I warned my client of the problem, but he wanted to go forward regardless of the price. The realtor kept quiet and did not appreciate my advice to the client. This appraiser is worth his weight in gold and I use no one else when the property is within the Southern California area.

Rule #7

"If any of the professionals tell you there's a problem with the purchase price, listen to them; it can save you a great deal of money."

The realtor involved in the purchase sought out a disreputable appraiser and got the value needed to close the deal. I did not fund the loan, and due to declining home prices the client now owes a mortgage that is approximately $100,000 more than the condo's current value.

The next chapter will familiarize you with the terms you will need to know when speaking with a loan officer. I gave them their own chapter because if you can talk the talk, the loan officers are less likely to try to mislead you. If they try to dazzle you with the lingo, you will know what they are talking about. Also, I always disliked referring to an index in the back of a book every time I need a reminder of a particular definition. We are now ready to start your journey in understanding the loan process and how to communicate with the loan officer to minimize the likelihood you will be misled by a dishonest lender or broker.

Chapter 2

The Mortgage Language: Why It's So Important

One of the best defenses against a loan officer's dishonesty is to understand the language of the mortgage industry. Without a basic knowledge of industry terms your lender or broker can talk you into submission, making the loan process so confusing or simplistic, as the case may be, that you run up the white flag and let them control the process.

This chapter will familiarize you with all the terms used in the loan process to enable you to communicate effectively and put your loan officer on notice that you know what you're talking about and that twisting words will not confuse you.

Many of the following terms will not be used in your discussion, but they are good to know for foundational purposes. The terms that have a "*" will be used in your discussion with the broker or lender.

Let's get started;

* **1003 (Mortgage Application):** This is the document that you will complete with your loan officer to submit to the underwriter for approval of your loan.

* **"A" Paper (Prime) Loans:** These loans are given to borrowers who have the best credit history and scores. The loan to value (LTV) can not exceed 80% or you may have to pay for mortgage insurance.

* **Annual Percentage Rate (APR):** This is the percentage rate that is a combination of your actual interest rate and the fees that your lender or broker charge that are paid for over the life of your loan.

Amortization Schedule: The complete schedule of your loan payments, showing how much interest and principal you are paying over the life of your loan. Early in the payment schedule most of your payment will go toward interest, while nearing the end of the payment period most of the payment will go towards principal.

Appraised Value: This is the value assigned by a licensed and authorized appraiser for your home. It is not the asking price or the actual sales price. The appraiser looks at sales comparables in your neighborhood over the past six months and assigns a value based on the building square footage, lot size, upgrades, number of bedrooms and baths, and so on.

Appraiser: A licensed or duly authorized individual who can assess the true value of a property.

* **ARM (Adjustable Rate Mortgage):** A mortgage with an interest rate that moves up or down, depending upon a chosen index. A margin is added to the index to indicate the current interest rate of the loan. Loans with short fixed periods are still considered ARMs.

* **ARM Margin:** This is a fixed percentage rate that is added to an index to show the real interest rate of an Adjustable Rate Mortgage.

Balloon Payment: These are large payments that are due from the borrower if the loan's amortization schedule exceeds the due date on the loan. A loan may be amortized over 30 years, to lower the payment, but due in 15 years, at which time it must be paid in full.

* **Closing:** This is the last step in the mortgage process, when the loan is funded and the transfer of title is recorded.

* **Closing Costs (Settlement Costs):** This is the total costs of your loan. It includes discount Points, origination fees, title fees, escrow fees and appraisal fee among others. You will receive an Est. HUD-1 at the time of your signing that estimates the closing fees. When your loan closes, you will receive a final HUD-1 showing the exact fees that were paid and loan amount that was borrowed.

Cloud on Title: This is any claim by a person, corporation or government entity that has some type of ownership interest in your home. These are usually discovered during the title company's title search and if a claim is discovered after closing, your title policy may cover any claims made on the title of your home.

* **Conforming Loan:** A mortgage that is equal to or less than the loan limits set by Fannie Mae and Freddie Mac, Government Sponsored Entities (GSEs). Loans that fall within their guidelines can be bought or insured by these GSEs. Recently, the limits have changed dramatically in high-cost areas.

Conventional Mortgage: A mortgage in which the terms and conditions meet the funding criteria of Fannie Mae and Freddie Mac. They can be fixed or adjustable rate mortgages. FHA and VA loans are examples of non-conventional loans.

* **Debt-to-Income Ratio (DTI):** This is a comparison between a borrower's overall monthly debt payments and their total monthly income. All the monthly debt payments are included such as, mortgage payment, property taxes, Homeowner's Insurance, credit cards, car payment, etc. DTI is vital in determining whether you qualify for a loan, since it shows the lender how likely you are to be able to repay your mortgage. The usual limit is 45% DTI, but there are lenders that vary this requirement depending on other factors.

* **Discount Points:** This is pre-paid interest that can be paid to lower the monthly interest rate on your loan. It generally costs 1% (1 Point) of your loan to lower your rate .125% to .25%, reducing your yearly interest rate and payments over the life of your loan. Many advertisements quote rates that come with large discount Points to get you to call. It can take many years to recoup the cost of paying discount Points.

Discount Rate: The interest rate charged by the Federal Reserve to banks for borrowing money from the government.

* **Earnest Money (Good Faith Deposit):** This is money deposited by a buyer into an escrow account, which demonstrates to the seller that the buyer is serious about the home purchase and allows time for the buyer to get financing for the purchase and inspect the home. It is held in a joint trust account, in many cases, with the buyer and seller having authority over the deposit. The amount required is determined by the seller and must be agreed to by the buyer.

Escrow: Escrow is a process that provides for a fair and equitable transfer of property from one person to another by a neutral third party (your escrow company) for the purchase of a home. A refinance is the transfer of a mortgage from one lender to another. Written instructions are received from the lender. When all instructions have been met, escrow will release all funds to the respective party.

Escrow Account: Also known as an impound account. This is an account that you can elect to have for your yearly taxes and homeowner's insurance to be paid monthly at same time you make your mortgage payment. It does require homeowners insurance and six months of taxes, on average, to be held in your account. California has a law against companies raising your interest rate if you decline escrow, while in other states you may have to pay .25% fee if you elect to pay your taxes and insurance separately.

Escrow Agent: An individual who has a fiduciary duty to all parties in a real estate transaction. They ensure that all documentation is correct and all the terms of the agreement have been met by all parties; buyer, seller, broker and lender prior to the closing of the transaction.

* **Equity:** The difference between the value of your home and the total balance of mortgages taken out on the home. If your home is appraised at $500,000 and your mortgage is $400,000, you have $100,000 in equity in your home.

FICO Scores (Fair Isaac Corporation): This is your credit score which is the product of your entire credit history being reported to the three credit bureaus (Experian, TransUnion and Equifax). It is a risk assessment that is assigned a number showing the lender how good or bad a credit risk you are.

Fixed Rate Loan: A loan whose interest rate is fixed for the entire term of the loan, usually 30, 20 or 15 years in length.

* **Float:** Floating a loan is used when the loan process has begun and you believe interest rates may fall, so you hold off on locking your rate until the rate goes

down. This can be risky, but a good loan officer will tell you if it is a good idea to float your rate.

* Homeowner's Insurance: This is a policy that the borrower obtains to insure their home against fire, theft and other damage to the property. It does not cover earthquake or flood insurance, unless your state requires it to be part of the policy. In most states you must purchase separate insurance to cover earthquake damage and the like.

* Index: A benchmark interest rate upon which adjustable rate mortgages are based. An adjustable rate mortgage is based on the current index and a margin that is added to the index to comprise your interest rate. The most commonly used indexes are:

> **Monthly Treasury Average (MTA):** Reflects the 12-month Treasury average based on average yields on US Treasury Securities made available by the Federal Reserve. Slow to move and lagging behind other indexes, it is a very stable index. Good if rates are climbing.

> **London Inter Bank Offering Rates (LIBOR):** The average interest rate on dollar-denominated deposits, traded between banks in London. It reflects world economic conditions. This index is far more volatile, moving up or down more quickly than other indexes. Good if rates are declining.

> **Certificate of Deposit Index (CODI):** 12-month average of the average yields on the nationally published 3-month Certificate of Deposits. This index moves slightly quicker than the other indexes. Good index if rates are declining.

> **11th District Cost of Funds Index ((COFI):** The weighted average of interest paid by the 11th District Federal Home Loan Bank District savings institutions for savings and checking accounts. ARMs tied to this rate rise and fall more slowly than the other indexes. Good if rates are climbing.

Jumbo Loans: This is a loan that exceeds the set conforming loan limits. These loans cannot be guaranteed by Fannie Mae or Freddie Mac. Since they cannot be bought or insured by these corporations, the rates on these loans will be significantly higher than on a conforming loan.

Loan Officer: This is a generic term that describes anyone able to take your loan information and begin the loan process. Many have broker or sales licenses, but if the are an employee of a corporation, they may not have any license at all.

* **Lock Period:** A specific time frame that confirms the interest rate that you have agreed upon. Available lock periods are 15, 30, 45 or 60 days. If your lock period is greater than 30 days, there will be an additional cost added to the interest rate for the longer lock period.

* **Loan to Value (LTV)/ Combined Loan to Value (CLTV):** LTV is the percentage of your 1st mortgage as compared to the value of your home. An example: your 1st mortgage is $400,000 and the value of your home is $500,000, your LTV is 80%. If you take out a 2nd mortgage on the same home for $50,000, then your CLTV would be 90%, combining the 1st and 2nd mortgages.

Mortgage: A debt instrument, or contract that is used to finance a home, using the property as collateral for the loan, with monthly payments to be made to pay back the loan. Until the debt is repaid in full, the lender is the lien holder on the property and may acquire the property if the borrower defaults on the loan.

Mortgage Broker: This is an individual or company that is an intermediary between a borrower and a lender. The broker will process the loan, but they do not have their own money to fund the loan. Currently, over 60% of loans funded in the United States are handled by brokers.

* **Negative Amortization:** A payment on your loan that doesn't pay the accrued interest and therefore increases the amount of principal on a monthly basis owed on your home.

* **Origination Points:** These are fees that your lender or broker charges to approve, process and fund your loan. They can include an origination fee, processing fee, lender fees, etc. All of these fees are considered pre-paid finance charges and are calculated as part of your APR. This is also referred to as the "front-end fee."

* **Par rate:** This is the rate at which the borrower pays no fee to buy down the interest rate and no YSP (rebate for a higher rate) for the funding of a loan. It is the best wholesale rate available on the market on the day you choose to lock your loan.

***Principal, Interest, Taxes & Insurance (PITI):** This is the total monthly cost of your home ownership. It includes the principal and interest on your mortgage loan, the yearly property taxes paid to the county and homeowner's insurance. The taxes and homeowner's insurance are divided into 12-monthly payments. This is critical for qualifying for a loan because your income vs. the PITI and other monthly debt payments you have will determine your Debt to Income Ration (DTI). It is the basis for the required reserves (savings and/or assets) that you must show the lender you have on hand. Usually two months to six months PITI is the required amount of reserves depending on the type of loan you choose.

* **Pre-Approved:** This entails the lender looking in-depth into your income, credit score and reserves to determine if you meet their lending requirements. If you have not yet chosen a home, a pre-approval can be obtained and this will tell you and your realtor the amount you can borrow from a particular lender.

* **Pre-paid Finance Charges (PFC):** These charges are required to be included in the APR calculation. They include all lender fees, broker fees, credit inquiry fee, pre-paid interest (discount points) and rebates received by the lender or broker. On the Good Faith Estimate, the PFC column should have a check mark to indicate it is included in the APR calculation.

* **Prepayment Penalty:** A clause in your mortgage loan contract (Note) that requires you to pay a fee if you were to sell or refinance your home during the fixed number of years that the contract states. The term of the penalty is set in writing, usually from 2 to 5 years. The penalty is calculated as a percentage of the loan amount, unless otherwise stated, with some additional mathematics involved. There are flat pre-pay fees that are usually attached to HELOCs and fixed 2nd mortgages.

Two Types of Prepayment Penalties

Hard Prepay: You will be assessed the penalty if you sell or refinance your home.

Soft Prepay: You can sell your home and not be subject to the penalty, but if you refinance, the penalty will be assessed.

* **Pre-Qualification:** This is an initial assessment of a borrower's ability to afford a home based on the borrower's representations of their income, assets, credit status and home value.

Private Mortgage Insurance (PMI or MI): This is private insurance that insures the lender against default, if you fail to continue making payments. PMI can be assessed against any conforming loan that exceeds 80% Loan to Value (LTV). The closer you are to 100% of your home's value, the higher the cost. It can be avoided by taking out a second mortgage on your home. Once your home's value has increased and the LTV drops below 80% PMI is no longer required (keep track of this yourself, as many lenders will not notify you that the PMI payment is no longer required). PMI is not insurance that protects the borrower.

Prime Rate: The interest rate that banks charge their most credit-worthy clients; they can be individuals, other lending institutions or corporations.

* **Rate Lock:** This is your ability to lock the rate that is available on any given day prior to the signing of your loan. If rates are expected to go up, it is a good idea to lock; if they are going down, you may want to float your rate and lock at a later date. A loan must be locked prior to the signing the loan documents.

* **Reserves:** This is a requirement by the lender that a borrower have a certain amount of money in savings to keep paying the loan if there is a loss in income for a period of time. The reserves required are based on you your monthly PITI (Principle, Interest, Taxes and Insurance payments). Most lenders require a minimum of 2 months of reserves and sometimes as much as 6 months.

* **Sub-prime Loans:** These are loans that carry higher interest rates due to the borrower's lack of credit-worthiness and the increased risk of the loan for the lender. The lower the FICO score, the higher the interest rate.

* **Title:** The right of ownership in a particular property. If there are no clouds on title, you are said to have "Good Title" to the property.

* **Title Insurance:** This is a policy that insures you and the lender against claims by third parties against the ownership of your home, such as a fraudulent transfer, lien or easement.

Trade lines: These are the actual credit lines (credit cards, auto loans, etc.) that have been extended to you and reported on your credit reports. Although the FICO score is vital to getting a good interest rate, if you do not have enough trade lines on your credit report, you may still not qualify for the best rates. Most "A" paper lenders require two 24-month and one 12-month trade line on your report. Some lenders don't require that your trade lines be active, but this is up to the specific lender.

Warehouse Line: This is a revolving line of credit in which a mortgage banker receives a loan from a lender. The note is kept with the lender and the mortgage banker then sells the loan on the secondary market.

* **Yield Spread Premium (Rebate):** This is a fee that is paid to a lender or broker for increasing the interest rate given to a borrower. The rebate is dependent upon how much the lender or broker raises the rate above the par rate, usually a .25% increase will give the lender or broker 1 Point. Sub-prime loans must be increased by .5% for the lender or broker to receive an extra Point on the loan. This fee is also referred to as "the back-end fee."

See, that wasn't too difficult. As we move along in this guide, refer back to this chapter to reinforce your understanding of the terms. We are going to move on to the loan process for a basic understanding of the roles played by your broker, lender, title and escrow companies and the time it takes to complete a loan.

Chapter 3

The Process & Players: Who Does What?

In this chapter I will explain the sequence of events that occur during your loan from interviewing your loan officer to closing, and the roles played by the different companies involved. Whether you're purchasing or refinancing, the process entails the same steps. Being prepared will relieve much of the stress associated with your loan.

There are important steps to take prior to speaking with any lender or broker. The most important of these is to obtain all three of your credit reports with scores. Federal law requires that you be given a free copy of your credit report one time per year from all three credit bureaus (Experian, TransUnion and Equifax). This free report will not contain your credit scores and you will need to pay for them to be able to speak with the loan officer.

You can order these comprehensive reports from any one of the three bureaus at www.experian.com, www.transunion.com and www.equifax.com. There are also many other websites that provide the same service, but you must make sure they are legitimate. You don't want to give your Social Security number to a fraudulent company only to risk identity theft.

These comprehensive reports (with scores) cost $40 to $50 depending upon the site you visit. Mortgage lenders do not consider your high score or low score; it is the mid-FICO score that all lenders consider when evaluating your credit worthiness. That's why it is important for you to have all three scores before contacting a broker. If you allow too many credit inquiries over an extended period of time, it may negatively affect your FICO scores. Your inquiry has no effect on your credit scores.

Rule #8

"Get all three of your credit scores before talking to a broker or lender; too many credit inquiries can have an adverse impact on your credit rating."

Review your pay stubs for an accurate assessment of your gross monthly income. Don't fudge on the numbers, you can include overtime and bonuses if you can prove you receive them on a regular basis. The best income records to check are your last two months pay stubs and the prior two years' W-2s. These are the income documents that most lenders will request. Your gross income will affect your Debt to Income Ratio (DTI) and the loan for which you qualify.

Once you have this information it is time to interview your prospective broker or lender. I suggest interviewing a minimum of three loan officers from various companies, even if your realtor, family member or friend refers you to a specific person. This is the most critical stage of your loan process, because if you pick the right individual to handle your loan, promises will be kept and deadlines will be met. In Chapter 8, I will detail all the questions that you will need answered and commitments you will need to request to make a good choice.

Most brokers and lenders think they are interviewing the borrower and this is the first sign that you're working with someone who is more interested in their needs than yours. If they are willing to answer your questions and give you a fair loan, let them know at the end of the conversation that if they keep their commitments to you, you will follow through with completing the loan. This is important because most loan officers have been misled by potential borrowers at some time in the past and they are skeptical of spending a great deal of time with someone who is just shopping rates.

Rule #9

"If the loan officer is not interested in answering your questions first, rather than getting answers from you, find another lender or broker."

When you are comfortable with your broker, this is the time to begin the application process. The first step is pulling your credit reports. Finding out where your mid-FICO score stands and how your credit looks overall is critical to qualifying for your loan. A loan application cannot be submitted to a lender without your credit history being included with the application.

The loan officer will ask you questions to complete the loan application, also called a 1003. Be ready to give them all employment and residency information for the past two years. Additionally, have your financial information ready, such as checking, savings, stocks, bonds and 401k information, as these will help you meet the reserve requirements. If you have all this information ready it will take as little as 30 minutes to complete the application process.

> "Federal Law requires that you receive a Good Faith Estimate and your APR within three days of submitting your loan application. Most loan officers will give you a GFE immediately, but most will never mention you are entitled to the APR."

The broker will then submit your application, credit report, GFE and a transmittal summary (containing the details of your loan) to the lender. Due to automated underwriting (software that takes the place of a manual underwriter) your pre-approval could take as little as a few minutes. If your loan must be manually underwritten it could take 2-5 days.

A competent broker will know from the start, if your loan will be approved. They will open up escrow for your loan. If it's a purchase, the seller will choose the escrow company, so the process will already have begun if you have signed a purchase contract. The broker will order escrow instructions, which will take 2-3 days to receive and at the same time a preliminary title report, which will take 3-5 days to receive. The broker or lender will also request an appraisal, which is dependent upon your availability, or your realtor's if it is a purchase. The appraisal will take 5-7 business days, so do not delay in setting your appointment. Once you see the time line below you will understand the importance of timely responses.

Rule #10

"Don't sign a purchase contract without prior approval for a loan."

While the broker is waiting for the appraisal, title and escrow instructions, he will receive your pre-approval with conditions. These conditions must be satisfied by you and submitted to the lender for final approval. There are "document" conditions (those needed by the lender prior to sending escrow the loan documents for signing) and "funding" conditions (those needed prior to the funding of your loan). Lenders and brokers will request all conditions at the beginning of the loan process.

Full document (Full Doc) loans require the most information. The following list will assist you and your broker in moving your loan to completion prior to your lock period expiring.

1. Pay stubs (last 2 months)
2. W-2s (last 2 years)
3. Bank statements (last 2 months)
4. Investments, if required for reserves (last quarterly statement)
5. Mortgage statement from prior lender (for pay-off information on a refinance)
6. Letter from landlord of "good payment history" for prior 2 years (first-time home buyer)
7. Homeowner's Insurance Declaration
8. Purchase Contract (if purchasing a home)
9. 1040 Tax filings (include Schedule C) for the last two years (if you are self-employed)
10. Current Property Tax Statement (if refinancing)

Having these documents ready prior to starting the loan process will reduce the stress related to the loan process. Again, being prepared will keep you, and not the loan officer, in charge of the loan process.

The following are documents provided by the broker and escrow that you must sign;

11. Borrower's Certificate and Authorization (a signed authorization allowing the credit inquiry)
12. Federal and State Disclosures
13. Mortgage Loan Origination Agreement (MLOA)
14. Signed Application (1003)
15. Escrow instructions (your escrow agent will mail you a copy for your signature)
16. Many states have their own forms that you must sign.

If you are purchasing a home, it is wise to get the application process started so that you can get pre-qualified for your home. This will allow the realtor to have greater bargaining power during the negotiation stage of your purchase. The pre-qualification letter will state the amount you qualify for based on the information you provided. It is important, as stated earlier, not to inflate your income or savings, because it can cause your loan to be denied during escrow if your records do not reflect the numbers you gave to the loan officer.

Now that the broker has the title report, escrow instructions and appraisal along with all the records stated above, he or she will submit the entire loan package to the lender. At this point the lender will have to manually underwrite your loan, insuring that the income, financial statements and property value supports the information you gave in your loan application. This process takes 3-5 days. Keep in mind that these are business days; lenders don't work on the weekends.

Once the underwriter has approved all of the document conditions, your loan will be placed in line for production of documents. Purchases have priority over refinances, so a refinance may take a little longer. The lender will forward all loan documents to the escrow agent, either by mail or email and you're ready to sign. If your loan has gone smoothly, you should have time and should insist upon the ability to review your documents prior to signing. Don't wait until the notary shows up to review your loan documents. You may feel pressured to complete the signing without thoroughly reading the terms and costs of your loan.

Rule #11

"Prior to signing your loan documents, have escrow email or overnight three key documents to you for review: the Note, Truth in Lending Statement and Estimated HUD-1."

The escrow agent has a fiduciary duty to you, and one of these duties is to disclose all available information including your loan documents. It is not unreasonable for you to request to see these documents prior to your signing date. In fact, it would be foolish not to request time to review the loan agreement. When it is time for signing, you will be buried with paperwork.

This is the most painful experience of the loan process, but if you have reviewed the Note, Truth in Lending Statement and Estimated HUD-1 prior to the signing date, your stress level will be diminished significantly. In Chapter 7, I will explain how to read these critical documents to ensure the rate and fees you were promised have not changed. If you intend to review your documents on the signing date, ask your loan officer to be available for questions.

If, after reviewing Chapter 7, you are not comfortable reading and interpreting the loan documents, you can visit www.mortgage-maze.net and I will review the key documents for you. The review will inform you of your interest rate, APR, total cost of your loan, whether you have a prepayment penalty and if so, how long the prepay period will last. Remember, these numbers are not set in stone, but we will show you how to prevent deception latter in this guide.

Now that you have reviewed your loan documents and are assured the rate and fees are correct, you can sign away. A notary will conduct the signing-either at the escrow office or a mobile notary can visit your home. Many borrowers want to ask the notary questions; but they are forbidden by law to explain the terms of your loan, so don't believe they are hiding something from you if they tell you they can't answer questions about the terms of your loan.

A purchase has no right of rescission. Once you have signed the loan documents, the loan can be funded the very next day (although this doesn't happen in most cases). A refinance, on the other hand, has a 3-Day Right of Rescission. This means the loan can be cancelled at anytime up to midnight on the third business day following the signing.

The "3-Day Right of Rescission" does not include Sundays, federal holidays and the day on which you sign. The following chart shows you the last day to cancel your loan following the signing. Remember, if there is a holiday, the rescission period will be extended for one day.

Signing Date	Right of Rescission Ends at Midnight
Monday	Thursday
Tuesday	Friday
Wednesday	Saturday
Thursday	Monday
Friday	Tuesday
Saturday	Wednesday
Sunday	Wednesday

If all funding conditions have been met, the loan will be placed in line for funding. This usually takes 1-4 days, depending upon the lender. On the day the loan funds, escrow will be notified and the funds will be disbursed. The mortgage will be recorded with the appropriate government entity (usually the County Recorder's Office) either on the signing date or the day after. Escrow has 48 hours to disperse any funds-to the borrower, if taking cash-out with a refinance, or to the seller, in a purchase transaction.

Rule #12

"If you are slow to respond to document requests, no one else is to blame if the loan does not fund on time or within your lock period."

The following table will give a general timeline for the processing of your loan. Any delay in responding to requests by any of the companies involved in the processing of your loan could not only delay your loan, but cost you more money by extending your lock period. In a purchase agreement with a 30-day escrow, the seller has the right to withdraw from the contract if the transaction has not been completed within that 30-day period. This usually does not occur, but it could, if the seller has received a higher offer and wants to receive more money for their home.

Table 3.1

Application	1 day
UW Review	1-5 days
Appraisal	3-7 days
Preliminary Title	1-3 days
Escrow Instructions	1-3 days
Signing Condition Review	2-4 days
In Line for Document Production	1-3 days
Signing	1-5 days
Right of Rescission (Refinance)	3 days (not including Sundays and Holidays)
Funding Condition Review	1-3 days
In Line for Funding	1-2 days
Recording	1 day

Total Timeline:	Purchase:	12-27 days
	Refinance:	15-30 days

If you have locked your loan for 30 days you can see how important it is to respond to all the document requests in a timely manner. Remember, these are business days. Many borrowers who believe they have plenty of time to finish their loan respond slowly to document requests and don't complete the process within the lock period. It is better to be prepared prior to starting the process than to try to find that pay stub you filed away in some lost file folder.

Chapter 4

Fees: Who Gets What

Borrowers are amazed at the number of fees associated with their loans. I am not defending the outrageous fees many lenders and brokers charge, but there is good reason why there are so many listed on your GFE and HUD-1. No matter what advertisement you have heard, no one does loans for free. When you think about how many individuals are actually working on your loan from all the different companies, it becomes clear that they all need to get paid. The average loan has 10-15 people working with the documents during the process. There are many individuals who work for the broker, lender, title company, escrow company and in some states attorneys, that have paperwork to review and produce for a loan's completion.

The question to ask yourself is, "Are all the fees reasonable?" This chapter will address the up-front fees (origination, title, escrow and appraisal) that are fixed and those that are variable. It will not discuss the hidden costs of your loan, that in combination with the up-front fees determine whether you are getting a good deal, or a bad one. The next chapter will discuss the hidden fees associated with your loan.

Rule #13

"Getting the lowest fees or the lowest rate doesn't mean you're getting the best loan; the two have to be looked at together."

Up-front Fees

Many books on the market today will tell you that the best way to compare loan costs is to get a GFE (Good Faith Estimate) from your lender or broker. This could not be farther from the truth. As mentioned before, most loan officers will say or do anything to get you started in the loan process with them. They know full well they do not intend to honor the GFE fees. By the time signing takes place, your fees and rate may change significantly and you will have tough choices to make. I will discuss the possible consequences of refusing to sign the loan in Chapter 8.

Rule #14

"The GFE (Good Faith Estimate) is not worth the paper it is printed on."

The GFE is an estimate and can be changed for a myriad of reasons. A dishonest loan officer will have multiple reasons why your fees or rate was raised by the time signing takes place. They should have pointed out the problems at the start, but many believe this would scare away a prospect. As an attorney, I believe these individuals should be held accountable for obvious bait-and-switch tactics, but proving "bad faith" is very difficult and not many attorneys are willing to file suit on a case that can be a financial loser for the lawyer. The borrower's only recourse is to report the company to the Federal Trade Commission or your states enforcement department. Don't hold your breath waiting for the government to come to the rescue. Both state and federal agencies are overwhelmed with complaints and they have no immediate action at their disposal to remedy your situation while the loan is in progress. If you believe that the actions taken by your lender or broker may have violated federal law; you can contact the Federal Bureau of Investigation's white collar crime unit.

Origination Fees

The origination fees, including all broker fees, lender fees, buy downs (discount fee), credit inquiry and any other fees that are charged by the broker or lender are called "pre-paid finance charges." Pre-paid finance charges are calculated into your APR (Annual Percentage Rate). The APR will give you the true cost of your loan, if all of these fees are checked as pre-paid finance charges on your

GFE. You can get a great interest rate, but if the fees associated with that rate are extreme, the loan may not be a fair deal. The higher the origination fees and discount Points, the higher the APR will climb over the interest rate offered to you.

Many lenders and brokers want you to pay an application fee. Although there are lenders that require brokers to pay this fee, it is only after a loan has been denied that the fee will be incurred by the broker. "Don't work with any lender or broker who attempts to get you to pay an application fee." If the broker is confident that your loan will be approved they won't ask you for this fee. This is a great way to force brokers and lenders to be honest with you about the chances of your loan being approved.

> "If your loan officer asks for an application fee; don't pay it. Find another lender or broker to finance your home."

Most consumers are aware that lenders and brokers charge origination fees that are expressed as "Points." One "Point" is equal to 1% of your mortgage loan; two "Points" is 2% of your mortgage loan amount, and so on. Additionally, there can be a processing fee, usually $500, and other fees that are tacked on to your loan by either the lender or broker. If you are working with a broker, you will pay their fees and lender fees. Lenders that supply wholesale products to brokers charge from $650 to as much as $1,100, and these fees are set in stone. Make sure your broker is including them on your GFE and they are identified as pre-paid finance charges.

You may jump to the conclusion that you should just go directly to a lender to cut out the middleman, but generally speaking, lenders will charge their retail customers more by offering brokers the par rate, thereby offsetting any savings that a borrower believes they will obtain. The par rate offered to brokers range from .25% to .5% less than the rates offered to consumers by a lender's retail office. Here is where a broker can save you on your rate and fees, if they choose not to mark up your interest rate to the retail rates offered by lenders.

Escrow Fees

Escrow agents have fixed costs included in your loan, such as the escrow fee (settlement fee), demand fee, courier or messenger fees, recording fee, attorney fee (if required by your state), check processing fee (if paying off credit cards and prior mortgage) and other little fees that can sometimes seem endless.

I am biased about the title and escrow company that I use because an escrow and title company that has both title and escrow under one roof is far less likely to increase their fees at signing. I have observed far too many times, borrowers being surprised at closing by fee increases that small escrow companies have a greater habit of attaching to your loan at the last minute. This is not the rule for smaller companies and they would object to my opinion, but I have had to pay for these costs too many times because my clients believe I should have protected them from these fee increases.

There are a slew of smaller fees such as, demand fee ($50), notary fee ($75-$150), title examination ($25), messenger ($10-20), electronic delivery ($75), recording fee ($50-150) and a fee for paying off credit cards in a refinance ($20 per creditor paid). The largest of the escrow fees is the settlement fee. If your state requires attorneys to handle your escrow, the fees could be significantly larger. The settlement fee is based on the loan amount and the following table (Table 4.1) gives you an example of settlement fees for different loan amounts.

Table 4.1

| | Escrow Settlement Fee | |
Mortgage Loan Amount	Refinance Fee	Purchase Fee
$100,000	$400	$400
$250,000	$400	$700
$500,000	$450	$1,200
$750,000	$500	$1,700
$1,000,000	$550	$2,200

Title fees

The largest title fee is for the title insurance. An owner's title insurance policy protects you against an individual who may claim some type of ownership interest in your home after the loan has been completed for as long as you or your heirs have an ownership interest in the property. A mortgagee's title insurance policy is usually taken out when a home is refinanced and protects the lender's interest in the home. Purchase policies are more costly than refinance policies. This is due to the greater likelihood of a claim being made against a property (such as an ownership interest, tax lien, mechanics lien or easement) after your purchase. California residents can visit www.titlewizard. com to compare the rates of various title companies. Residents of other states can visit www.easytitlequote.com for an estimate from a title company in your area. Be careful, ask for all the fees, many title companies will quote a low cost policy only to add other fees to make up for the loss. The following table gives you some idea of the cost of the title insurance (see Table 4.2), but they do vary greatly from one title company to another.

Table 4.2

Loan Amount	Settlement Fees Purchase Policy (Cost)	Refinance Policy (Cost)
$250,000	$1,058	$625
$500,000	$1660	$900
$750,000	$2,160	$1,150
$1,000,000	$2,660	$1,250

Rule #15

"The fixed title and escrow fees should be included in your GFE; if not, find another loan officer."

Many lenders and brokers produce GFEs that fail to add the title and escrow fees. The loan officer will purposely omit these fees to make the loan more appealing at the outset, only to state at signing that they didn't know the escrow and title fees at the time they gave you a GFE. If you believe this, let me tell you what kind of cheese the moon is made out of. I have been working with the same escrow agent for the last three years and he is always within $250 of his estimate when it comes time to close the loan. In an industry that seems to think money grows on trees, it is good to have a solid relationship with an escrow agent and title officer that you can count on. If they were to change their fees with every loan, that reflects on me, because no matter the reasons given by a title or escrow company for increased fees, I am responsible for giving my clients the correct information.

Generally, title and escrow fees will range from $1,500 to $2,500 on a refinance, and on purchases they will range from $2,200 to $3,500 for the buyer. Remember, it's ultimately your lender or broker that must make certain the other service providers are doing their job professionally and they must stand behind their fee estimates. You can compare title and escrow companies, but you will not see their fees until signing unless you ask for an exact accounting before choosing their company. Many brokers and lenders work with specific title companies and can get discounted rates if they give them enough loans each month.

You may encounter title companies that will charge less for the title insurance, but they invariably make up for it with other charges. Again, take them as a whole, not one charge at a time. These fees are usually non-negotiable.

Non-fixed Fees

I know this chapter seems endless, but we're almost at the finish line. There is one non-fixed fee that is listed on your HUD-1 that is determined by the date on which your loan funds. When refinancing or purchasing a home, you have to pay interest on your loan beginning on the funding date. The daily interest will be calculated from the funding date to the end of the month and will be included in your loan costs. Since no one can be sure of the exact date your loan will fund, the broker can only estimate the daily interest. Make sure this was included in your GFE; it will be item 901.

Borrowers who are refinancing will have two interest payments included in their loan. The first is to the prior lender, who will be paid their daily interest rate up until the funding date of your new loan. The second is the same as with a purchaser-the daily interest accrued from the funding date to the end of the month. The escrow agent is required to calculate the correct amount. If your prior lender has been overpaid they will forward a refund to you, usually within 30 days.

As an example, if your loan funds on the 15th of the month and the interest on your loan will total $2,000 a month, the loan will include a daily interest rate cost of $1,000. If your loan funds nearer the end of the month, this payment will be smaller; if at the beginning of the month, it will be larger.

For first-time home buyers and those who own and have forgotten, when your first statement arrives you are paying, unlike rent, for the prior month. It will take the lender time to transfer your loan to the servicing department and get the first statement out to you, so you get to skip a month. For example, if your loan funds in the middle of January, your first mortgage payment will be due on March 1st. It's that simple. This is another way that unscrupulous lenders and brokers make you think they are doing you a favor. I have had multiple clients tell me other brokers will make their first mortgage payment for them (because you get to skip a month prior to making your first payment). This is just not true.

Rule #16

"If your loan officer tells you will get to skip a month on your mortgage payment because they will pay it for you, run; this is one of the most blatant lies in the industry."

Property Taxes & Homeowner's Insurance

The last two fees that are determined during the loan process are your homeowner's insurance and property taxes. If purchasing a home, the lender will require that you have a homeowner's policy paid for the entire year. Shop around for a good homeowner's policy, as polices can vary as much as $1,000 between different insurance carriers. You will also have to pay the property taxes on your home from the date of closing. The taxes may not be on your GFE because the escrow agent estimates the monthly taxes. Property taxes vary greatly from state to state. Your tax preparer should be able to estimate this for you prior to purchasing a home. These estimates are important because taxes and insurance are part of the PITI that determines how large a loan you can afford and the reserves that will be required.

If the purchase price is higher than the price the prior owner paid for the property, be ready to receive a Supplemental Tax request a few months down the road asking for an additional tax payment. The escrow agent will estimate taxes based on the prior owner's tax rate, not on your purchase price. The County will reassess your taxes and ask for a supplemental tax payment. A home's assessed value will not change if refinancing a property.

You will be given the option to open up an escrow account (taxes and insurance will be added to your monthly payment). If you choose to have an escrow account your lender will have you place money in the account. The drawback to placing money in an escrow account is that you increase your out-of-pocket costs. In addition, you will also make monthly payments to your lender for the taxes and insurance. To put it simply, you have made a loan to your lender for which you are not receiving any interest.

Escrow accounts are a good way for borrowers to budget their money, but it does cost you a little for the service. Another reason to open an escrow account is to save the increased fee to your rate (usually .25% YSP for most lenders) associated with paying your taxes and insurance yourself. Only California prohibits this fee for non-escrowed loans.

Chapter 5

The Hidden Cost of Your Loan

Yield Spread Premium or Rebate

As I have explained in the prior chapter, many of your fees will be seen on your GFE at the beginning of the process and on the estimated HUD-1 which you receive on the day of your signing. What you may not see is a cost built into the rate you received, where the lender or broker receives a YSP (Yield Spread Premium), as it is called in the industry. Brokers and lenders make this rebate by increasing your interest rate above the par rate. Consumers who are not aware of the YSP do not understand that it is costing them thousands in unnecessary interest payments. Many who are aware of the rebate call it a "kickback" and believe there is something illegal about it. It is not illegal, but this hidden rebate does invite misrepresentation and unless your lender or broker advises you of its existence he or she is not being honest with you.

As few as 1 out of 100 borrowers know what a YSP is and how it affects your interest rate. The average US homeowner pays more per month than was necessary, because their lender or broker failed to mention that they received thousands of dollars for inflating an unsuspecting consumer's interest rate over the best interest rate available. In the end, the consumer simply ends up with a higher monthly mortgage payment.

Wholesale Rate Sheet

Table 5.1 illustrates how an "A" paper lender would show their rates to a broker. Lenders and mortgage bankers, as mentioned earlier, do not have to disclose the YSP on the HUD-1 or in the APR calculation. The rate sheet shows the large fees that a broker or lender can add to your loan without your knowledge if they can successfully hide this from you. The estimated rebate in dollars is based on a loan amount of $400,000. The actual rebate dollar amount is calculated by multiplying the percentage and loan amount. If the loan amount is smaller or larger than our example, the actual dollar amount will decrease or increase accordingly. You have heard me mention the par rate (it is defined in Chapter 2); but here we can see how the YSP is calculated giving your lender or broker an avenue to increase their income at your expense. In Table 5.1 rebates that have a "-" in front of them indicate the broker is getting paid for giving you a higher rate. A positive number indicates a buy down cost to the borrower.

Table5.1

Wholesale Rate Sheet (30-Year Fixed Loan: $400,000)			
Rate	30-Day Lock	45-Day Lock	60-Day Lock
6.125%	0.041	0.168	0.291
Buy Down Cost	$164	$672	1,164
6.25%	-0.412	-0.267	-0.198
Rebate	$1,640	$1,068	$792
6.375%	-0.822	-0.697	-0.572
Rebate	$3.288	$2,716	$2,288
6.5%	-1.226	-1.141	-1.016
Rebate	$4,904	$4,564	$4,240

Table 5.1 illustrates how a small increase to your rate can place thousands of dollars in the pocket of your lender or broker. What usually happens in a volatile market is that borrowers don't know the par rate on any given day and the rate offered to them may sound good when a loan officer recommends locking their loan. The loan officer will tell you rates are great today and he can get you a 6.5% interest rate on your loan with a 30-day lock.

It may sound reasonable considering rates have been jumping all over the place in the last few weeks, so you decide to grab it while it's down. You lock your loan and start moving forward with the process, but what you didn't know and the loan officer didn't disclose to you, is that he just made $4,904 in additional fees by giving you the 6.5% interest rate (Table 5.1 assumes a $400,000 loan). This is an extra 1.22 Points in fees. If the lender or broker has charged you 1 Point up-front, the total fees on your loan will be 2.22 Points or $8,880; which is usually far more than the agreed upon fees.

You will be paying for the rebate each month as you make a higher loan payment due to the higher interest rate. You could have received the same loan at 6.25% with very little rebate to the broker if he or she was being honest with you. The only way to protect yourself against this fraud is to know the par rate on the day you lock your loan. You can check today's par rate by visiting www.mortgage-maze.net to see today's par pricing.

Rule #17

"A slightly higher rate above the par rate can put thousands of dollars in your lender's pocket while you have to pay for it in a higher interest rate."

Checking Daily Interest Rates

Interest rates change daily and sometimes multiple times per day, so you must check them accordingly to see what the lowest available rates are throughout the day. This is difficult because many websites that pretend to be a consumer-oriented website receive fees from the lenders who advertise on their sites. Most of the rates are completely without a factual basis. You must be aware that any website that accepts advertising dollars to post rates is not going to be watching the rates that are offered. The low rates on these websites are not available unless you pay huge fees for the discounted rates, so don't waste your time calling these companies; they will more than likely change your rate and fees when it comes time for signing. Try to get straight answers from some of these loan officers; it will be a frustrating experience. If they can't be honest at the beginning of the process, there is no reason to believe they will keep their commitments later.

> "Websites that represent themselves as consumer information resources that have rates advertised on their site are no friend of the consumer. These sites accept large fees from lenders to post interest rates that have no basis in reality. Consumers will pay huge fees to get the rates quoted on these sites."

There are a few websites that really try to give you the average rates available at any given time. Freddie Mac's website, www.freddiemac.com/dlink/html/PMMS/display/PMMSOutputYr.jsp will give you the average rates for the past week, but this doesn't tell you what the rates are today, and on average the rates are not as accurate as you would like them to be, since they conduct a survey of what lenders and brokers are actually giving their clients. Additionally, the rates are the average of both conforming and jumbo loans which are very different from one another. Remember, most of these lenders and brokers are increasing your interest rate to charge you a YSP and they may lie to the person conducting the survey, which should come as no surprise.

The best website to visit is www.mortgage-maze.net for updated par rates. We will keep you informed of the changing market conditions giving you the knowledge you need to receive the very best rates on any given day. You must know the par rate before speaking with a loan officer or you will be defenseless against the myriad of sales pitches thrown at you during the initial conversation.

Direct lenders do not have to disclose the YSP on their GFE or Truth in Lending Statement, and neither do brokers who are correspondents or have warehouse lines with a particular lender. The loan officers that are required to disclose the rebate are brokers who are not mortgage bankers. This is a great argument to work with a small broker and let him know you are aware of YSPs and how they affect your rate. A good broker will charge no more than 1.5 Points on an "A" Paper loan-that is origination and YSP fees combined. If you're paying more than this, find another broker. Many brokers will consider handling your loan for as little as 1 Point, in total, if the loan is larger than $300,000.

> "Direct Lenders, correspondent brokers and brokers with warehouse lines do not have to disclose the YSP (rebate) they are making on your loan. Federal law does not require disclosure that they have raised you interest rate above par. Only brokers that are not described above must disclose the YSP they receive."

As pointed out in Chapter 1, lenders have spent millions in Washington D.C. to ensure consumers have no idea what they are really paying for your loan. It's worth repeating, Federal law requires brokers to disclose the rebate they receive, so any increase over the par rate will be shown on the Est. HUD-1 that consumers receive at signing. Lenders make thousands in fees, while consumers are left in the dark praying that they're not being taken to the cleaners on their loan. Amazingly, the law requires that the YSP be placed in the HUD-1's column where the description of the fees is located, not in the borrower's (buyer's) cost column. The law was actually written to allow brokers some way of hiding this cost and many consumers won't catch it unless they read their documents carefully.

Sub-prime borrowers usually have to pay more for their loan and are targeted by the worst predators in the industry. A general rule for those who have less than perfect credit is; to pay no more than 2 Points for your loan and don't fall for the belief that the loan officer is doing you a favor. As lending guidelines become more restrictive, brokers will have to work harder to find a lender who will fund a sub-prime loan.

Rule #18

"If your broker tells you that the fee he receives from the lender is not costing you anything, move on to an honest broker."

When using a direct lender, broker correspondent or broker with a warehouse line, you will never be sure what you paid for your YSP unless you do your homework. I may be biased, but the small broker, who is dependent on referrals from his or her local market, may give you the edge you need to avoid hidden costs in your loan. Working with a broker in your area will also give you the ability to bring a small claims action against them at your local courthouse to recover any surprise fees that occur at closing.

Finding Out How Much Your Loan is Costing You

There is a way to find out exactly how much your broker is really making on your loan, both up-front fees and rebate. Visit us at www.mortgage-maze.net and use the APR calculator as described below to determine the true cost of your loan.

> ➢ While working with a lender, generally you can assume they are charging you at least 1 Point that they are not disclosing to you. Additionally, they will not lower their interest rates even if you point out to them that the par rate is .25% lower than the best rate they are quoting you. If you are working with a direct lender, look at the par rate located on www.mortgage-maze.net and for each .25% increase over par they are offering you, add 1 Point (1%) of the loan amount to your costs. As has been stated above, this cost will not be part of the APR calculation. Interest rates that are more than .25% above the par rate are too costly if you are already paying a Point in origination fees. I strongly suggest you go to a broker because they can't hide the YSP; you just have to make sure they know you are aware of the game that is played with these fees.

To accurately determine the real cost of your loan, go to the above website, once you have your rate and APR from your loan officer (don't move forward with your loan until they give you a Truth in Lending Statement that has the APR). Using the calculator…

- ➤ Plug in your loan amount and rate;
- ➤ Remove the 1 Point from the "origination fee percentage" box;
- ➤ Remove the 1 Point from the "Points paid" box;
- ➤ Add fees to your loan in one of the "other fees to include" box, using $1,000 increments;
- ➤ Hit the "Calculate" button;
- ➤ Repeat the last two steps until the APR on the calculator matches the APR from the Truth in Lending Statement you received from the loan officer.

This is the total cost of your loan. If you agreed to buy down your interest rate, make sure to subtract that fee after you have determined the total cost of your loan. You now know how to find the true costs of your loan. If the loan officer is charging you more than the combined fee that you agreed to, move on to another lender or broker. Don't waste your time negotiating with a dishonest loan officer; you're throwing away more of your valuable time and money. Soon after the publication of this guide, there will be a new calculator that requires you submit your loan amount, interest rate and APR and it will give you the total pre-paid finance charges associated with your loan.

Chapter 6

Qualifying for Your Loan; How Your Rates are Determined

The Mortgage Bond Market

The first factor that determines the interest rate you can receive is based on what is available in the market. This is the one factor that is totally out of your control. Mortgage loans are sold on what is called the secondary market, where investors purchase loans in large groups to earn a return on their money. "A" paper conforming loans that meet Fannie Mae and Freddie Mac guidelines are purchased by these two entities. All other loans are purchased by individual investors, corporations and other lending institutions. The riskier the loan, the higher return these investors demand. Therefore the higher interest you will pay if you are considered a high-risk borrower for reasons I will discuss below.

A novel could be written on how the market determines rates, but I will address some general thoughts on the matter. Most of the time, bad economic news for the economy has the affect of lowering long-term interest rates. A poor economy means lower inflation and investors don't have to be concerned with inflation eating up all their interest. The opposite is also true, for the most part; inflation will induce higher interest rates because investors want their investment returns to outstrip inflation. There are other determiners, such as the cost of less risky treasury bonds, how the stock market is performing, how much foreign investment is flowing into mortgage bonds. China and Saudi Arabia hold huge portfolios of our mortgage bonds.

> "The Federal Reserve lowering the Discount Rate; does not directly affect long-term interest rates. Many lenders will use this as a means to get you to call them, even though long-term rates have not changed."

Just to dispel a myth, the Federal Reserve lowering the Discount Rate does not necessarily mean mortgage rates will go down; there is no direct affect. Rates may be affected indirectly, but many times a lower Discount Rate will push mortgage rates higher. Lowering the discount rate tends to invite inflation and this is the enemy of the mortgage bond market. Investors are always looking down the road, not just for their return on investment over the next few months. Your loans don't mature for 30 years, which is a long time to wait, if inflation is on the rise.

Rule #19

"All lenders and brokers get their money from the same market."

A particular lender may have a slightly better rate with one loan product vs. another. It depends upon the type of loans their particular investor are more interested in purchasing. Those loans purchased or insured by Fannie Mae and Freddie Mac will usually have the lowest interest rates available.

Now, I will move on to the factors that you control; these are the risk factors that lenders will look at to determine if you are "A" paper, Alt-A or a Sub-prime ("Expanded" as it is beginning to be called) borrower. Sub-prime has a demeaning connotation to it, so the industry is starting to refer to the loans as expanded products.

Your Credit (FICO Scores & Credit History)

Credit scores are the most important factor in determining what rate you will qualify for with any loan that you choose. The mortgage industry depends upon

the three major credit bureaus, Experian, TransUnion and Equifax, to determine your credit worthiness. It is not the high or low score that is important,
but the middle score that lenders rely on to qualify you for a loan program.

Rule #20

"Pull all three of your credit reports and FICO scores prior to speaking with a lender or broker."

If you have a 740 mid-FICO score, this will qualify you for any product that is
available on the market, so long as other factors discussed below do not disqualify you. A 680 mid-FICO score will generally qualify you for the best rates, but
it may cost you a little in an added fee to get the par rate. All lenders have a tier
system (every 20 points) and the lower your FICO score the higher your interest rate will climb. Scores below 680 can still qualify for good rates, but there
can be added hits (costs) to a particular rate if your score is 679 or below.

Alt-A loans are for borrowers with less than perfect credit scores that have not
fallen below 620. Generally, any mid-FICO that falls below 620 would now be
considered sub-prime. The product (loan) guidelines are constantly changing
so what may be considered Alt-A this year could be sub-prime next year. It is
dependent on how tight or loose money is at the time of your loan, the market
will determine how borrowers are categorized.

Beyond your credit score is the actual information contained in your credit
report. You can have a 700 FICO score, but only one trade line (creditor you
have an open account with) and this will probably disqualify you from any
loan. Most lenders, even those who offer sub-prime products, require a certain
number of open or closed trade lines on your credit report. Generally speaking,
two 24-month lines and one 12-month line will ensure your credit history supports a good loan if your scores are high enough. Some lenders don't require
that all the accounts reported on your credit history be currently open at the
time you seek a loan. If they were closed within the last seven years, they should
still be on your credit report and may be counted as a trade line by the lender's
underwriter.

The only way to avoid the higher rates associated with a sub-prime loan is to
improve your credit to qualify for the best rates available. Many borrowers

are the victims of collection companies that routinely violate the Fair Credit Reporting Act, by continuing to report obsolete information as current derogatory accounts. I have years of experience representing clients that have been the targets of these companies. Federal law states that derogatory marks on your credit can be reported for seven years, unless you have a bankruptcy, lien or judgment which can remain on your credit for ten years. Generally, collectors and creditors have four years to file a claim in court against you, but many do not since the debts are small and it is not worth the legal fees to attempt to collect. So, they change the date of "last activity" to continue to damage your credit scores in the hopes of forcing you to pay. Many of these companies tell borrowers that if they pay their old debt it will help their FICO scores. Nothing could be further from the truth. If you have a very old debt, by making a payment, you have moved the date of "last activity" to the payment month and your FICO score will actually go down.

A whole book could be written on your rights as a consumer, but is far beyond the focus of this guide. The laws actually have strong incentives for creditors and collection companies to follow the law, including punitive damages that can be awarded for violations of the federal credit laws. If you have been the victim of credit reporting fraud, contact a local consumer rights attorney in your area to see if you have legal remedies to your problem.

Debt to Income Ratio (DTI)

You can have great credit scores, but be so buried in debt that your monthly payments to creditors combined with your mortgage payment, taxes and insurance will make it impossible to qualify for a loan. This is called your Debt to Income Ratio (DTI); it is a important determiner of whether or not your loan is approved.

DTI takes into account all your monthly debt payments, credit cards, car loans, mortgage, property taxes, and homeowner's insurance and expresses them as a percent of your total income. For example, if you make $5,000 per month and you credit card payments are $500/month and your mortgage, taxes and insurance total $2000/month, your DTI would be 50%. The total monthly debt in this case is half of the borrower's gross income. It doesn't mean they would be disqualified from a loan, but they may have to pay a higher rate due to the added risk of their loan.

Most "A" Paper loans require a DTI equal to or less than 45%. There are exceptions, but Fannie Mae and Freddie Mac will not purchase loans with a DTI greater than 45%. Some sub-prime lenders will go as high as 55%, but recently the number of these lenders has diminished, and if the market continues on its current course they will no longer exist in a year or two. Generally, FHA loans require a DTI of 43% or less, but there are exceptions if the lenders automated underwriter accepts the loan due to the strength of other factors.

Many self-employed borrowers have difficulties qualifying for loans because most lenders will ask to see their Schedule "C" tax filing and determine the DTI based on their income after deductions. This was the original purpose for the stated income loans, but these stated loans have been abused by lenders over the past few years, contributing to the collapse of the housing market and lending industry.

Types of Loans (Fixed, Adjustable and Others)

The length of time the loan rate remains fixed can have a significant impact on the rate that you receive. Most mortgages are based on a 30-year amortization schedule, except for 15-year and 20-year fixed loans that are based on a shorter amortization schedules; these have much higher payments associated with them since you're paying off the loan sooner. This schedule is the length of time it will take to pay off the entire principal of your loan. There are always new products being introduced that are variations on the more simplistic loan schedules.

The following list represents the most frequently used loans in the mortgage industry:

1st Mortgages
➤ 30-Year Fixed
➤ 40-Year Fixed (most have a balloon payment at 30 years)
➤ 2/28 (Fixed for 2 years, then adjustable in the following years)
➤ 3/27 (Fixed for 3 years, then adjustable in the following years)
➤ 5/25 or 5/1 ARM (Fixed for 5 years, then adjustable in the following years)
➤ 7/1 ARM (Fixed for 7 years, then adjustable in the following years)

> ➤ 10/1 ARM (Fixed for 10 years, then adjustable in the following years)
> ➤ 15 Year Fixed (Fully amortized over 15 years)
> ➤ 20 Year Fixed (Fully amortized over 20 years)
> ➤ Interest Only (Many of the above loans can have an interest-only period. Be warned, if you make the interest-only payment, when this period comes to an end, your loan will be recast with a shorter amortized period and your payments will increase significantly).
> ➤ Option ARM/Pick a Pay (This gives you a choice of payments each month, usually 15-year amortized, 30-year amortized, 30-year interest-only and the teaser payment that is a negative amortized payment). This loan will be discussed in great detail later in this chapter due to the risks involved.
> ➤ Federal Housing Administration (FHA) Loans
> **2nd Mortgages**
> ➤ Fixed 2nd Mortgages (Used to avoid Mortgage insurance, and amortized over 30-years with a balloon payment in the 15th year)
> ➤ Home Equity Line of Credit or HELOC (2nd mortgage with the rate tied to the Prime Rate and has an interest-only payment). This loan has a balloon payment in year 15.

While determining what type of loan you wish to have there are significant risk factors that can help you in your decision-making process. Let's talk about the benefits and risks of these loans.

Fixed Loans

Fixed loans are the safest from the standpoint that your payments will never change. Borrowers on a fixed income who believe that they will stay in their home for seven years or more will find this loan to be the best option. Rates on this type of loan have ranged from 5% to 8% over the past eight years for "A" paper borrowers. These rates are historically low and currently attractive to many borrowers. The other benefit is that you won't have to refinance in a few years, as opposed to an ARM (Adjustable Rate Mortgage) where the rate may jump at the end of the fixed period and you will either pay a higher interest rate or have to refinance. Why give the lenders and brokers more money to refinance, when that money could have been used to pay down your mortgage?

Rule #21

"Be aware that most loans are amortized over 30 years; make sure it is a 30-year fixed loan."

The drawback to the fixed rate mortgage is that the interest rate can be much higher than for a shorter fixed period. This is not always true, especially during the last ten years when the margins between fixed and ARM loans were not that significant. The market will control what happens in the future, and it pays to investigate the difference between these rates. Your lender or broker will let you know the difference, but you must look at the rates yourself to ensure you are not being misled.

Adjustable Rate Mortgages (ARMs)

If you choose an ARM product you may be able to enjoy a lower interest rate for a period of time; but once it goes adjustable, be ready for your interest rate to jump. The rate that you will pay after your loan moves into its adjustable period will usually be greater than the fixed rate that was available when you received your loan. All ARMs come with a lifetime cap on the rate, but these are extremely high and if the index that the loan is tied to increases significantly, so will your payments.

Many of the ARM loans are tied to specific indexes during their adjustable periods. These indexes are the LIBOR, COFI, CODI and MTA (defined in Chapter 2). You can look on the internet to see the historical averages for the index and ensure that they have not seen dramatic increases over the last ten or twenty years. The adjustable rate will also have a "margin" that is determined by the lender and will be buried in your loan documents. Over the past few years many margins averaged 2.5%. As an example, if your loan is tied to the LIBOR index and it is at 5.5%, and your margin is 2.5%, your interest rate will be 8%. No one knows where these indexes will be in five or seven years, so make sure you are willing to take this risk of an ARM, or be ready to refinance to a fixed loan at a higher interest rate a few years down the road.

Borrowers must make their own choice of whether to have a fixed or ARM product. There are a few considerations that everyone must weight in deciding which is best for their particular needs. Sometimes there is very little difference between the rates, so opting for an ARM may make little sense due to the risk of higher interest rates within a few months or years. The spread can be quite large at some points, but changes to the indexes can occur rapidly and perceived savings can therefore disappear just as fast. If you are forced to refinance in a few years, moving to a lower fixed interest rate, the cost to refinance may eat up much of the savings you gained in prior years. Lenders and brokers would like everyone to choose ARM products, since the likelihood that you will refinance again in the coming years is much greater.

Sub-prime borrowers who opted for a 2/28 or 3/27 loan may not be able to refinance into a fixed rate loan if their home does not appreciate in value and they had a high LTV to begin with. This is a trap that many have fallen into and are now facing foreclosure because they are unable to pay the high interest rates that associated with the adjustable period of their loan.

Option ARM (Pick a Pay) Loan

I want to take time out and explain one of the most deceptive loans on the market, the Option ARM. A whole book could be written about this loan, its impact on homeowners and the housing market itself. I believe that more foreclosures will be caused by this loan than any other available on the market.

This loan when explained by an experienced (with highly questionable integrity) loan officer will sound great at the outset of your decision-making process. The only borrowers that this loan may be a plausible choice for are individuals that have dramatic swings in their monthly income or investors that are speculating on appreciation in the housing market. The speculators are no longer in the market for obvious reasons.

The Option ARM will give you a choice, on a monthly basis, of making four payments toward your loan. These are a 30-year fully amortized payment, a 15-year fully amortized payment, a 30-year interest-only payment and a teaser payment (1%-2%) that is a negatively amortized payment. Lenders and brokers make bushels of money off of this loan by charging you rebate Points that will increase the margin on your loan and the length of your pre-payment penalty period. Another reason why this loan is a favorite of lenders and brokers is that you can qualify for your home based on the teaser rate, so if you don't have the income to support another type of loan, they can get you qualified for this loan, even though you can't afford the interest-only payment.

Rule #22

"The Option ARM Loan is the most costly, risky and dangerous mortgage to select when purchasing or refinancing your home."

In my years as a mortgage broker I have never suggested or funded an Option ARM loan. If I am going to keep my clients interests as my top priority, this is not the loan. If you are working with a loan officer who is pushing this loan, I strongly suggest you find another lender or broker.

Rule #23

"The real beneficiaries of the Option ARM loan are lenders and brokers who make thousands without you knowing about it."

The lowest payment that gets every borrower's heart pumping is incredibly appealing. This is the teaser rate, usually a 1% or 2% payment. For example, on a $400,000 loan the payment can be as little as $1286 (1%). Wow, you can have a really nice home for that low payment, right? Not really. If you continue to make this payment over a year or two, the equity in your home will disappear because this is a negative amortized (Neg. Am.) payment. What this means is that your true interest rate is much higher than the teaser payment, and the difference in interest between the teaser payment and the real interest rate will be added onto the principal owed on your home.

> "If you make the Option ARM teaser payment, the difference between that payment and the interest-only payment will be added onto the principal of your home; effectively, giving away the equity you have in your home."

Let me give you an example of how this works. Let's say the interest only-payment is at 6% on your loan and the mortgage balance is $400,000. The teaser payment is $1,286/month (1%). The interest-only payment would be $2,000/month. In this example, you will be adding $714/month onto your principal by making the teaser payment. This is the definition of a Neg. Am. payment. If you continue to make the teaser payment, in one year you will have lost $8,784 in equity of your home. You can see how foreclosure is only months away.

What is even more horrible about this loan is that the loan limits the number of teaser payments you can make by either capping at the value of your home or a specified percentage over the original loan amount, such as 5%, 10% or 15%. While you are happily making this low payment for a couple of years, you will soon receive a letter from your lender that informs you that you are no longer allowed to make this payment and must make an interest-only payment at a minimum. Once you have reached the teaser payment cap, your loan will recast (the new mortgage payment will be recalculated based on the current principal owed on the loan), if it hasn't done so already; and your payments will shoot like a rocket skyward.

Most of the Option Arm loans will recast at a 6-month or 12-month interval. So as you make the teaser payment, the difference between this payment and the interest-only payment will continue to grow. I have refinanced many clients out of these loans to help them save their homes. Cam Kenady, one of my clients said, "When we purchased our condo the loan officer at a national lender made this loan sound so appealing and he never told us that the interest rate and payment would continue to increase because it was an adjustable rate loan. It only took us three months to figure out we had been misled and had to get out of it, even though there was a large prepayment penalty."

Here is the pitch you will hear from your loan officer; "This is a great loan because you can make a small payment or a larger payment depending on how your finances are in any given month. Just choose the interest-only payment to avoid any more principal owed on your home (if they are nice enough to mention the Neg. Am. issue)." As stated above, if you qualified for this loan based on the teaser rate, it is very likely that once your ability to make this payment disappears, you will not be able to afford your home. Think about this for a moment; if you must pay an interest-only payment to just break even on your loan, why choose an adjustable rate mortgage in the first place. You are much better off choosing a 30-year interest-only loan (with a 10-year interest-only period) than setting yourself up with a risky loan such as the Option ARM. I believe this loan will no longer be available on the market within a year or two because although it allows the profit margins of lenders to look good this year, when the loan adjusts, many borrowers will face foreclosure and the company's bottom line will suffer in the coming years.

Rule #24

"If you can't qualify for a loan based on a 30-year amortized payment; you do not belong in the home."

To put this in perspective, loan officers just want to sell you a loan; most don't care if you lose your home in couple of years. They still got paid. Many brokers have lost their right to submit loans with particular lenders because the default rates (foreclosures) on their loans were too high. It is amusing to see lenders that pushed these loans claiming that it is the broker's fault. The whole industry should be ashamed of itself, as the current housing crises can be laid at the feet of the brokers and lenders that misled homeowners into choosing the Option ARM, because it is responsible for a large portion of the foreclosures that are occurring today.

Federal Housing Administration (FHA) Loans

FHA loans are mortgages that are insured by the Federal Housing Administration and must meet the lending criteria of the FHA. Over the past few years these loans were not as attractive to homeowners and buyers because the interest rates offered were higher than those in the conventional market. In addition, consumers have to pay a mortgage insurance premium up-front that ranges from 1.25% to 2.25% of the loan amount. FHA also requires a monthly mutual mortgage insurance payment, so long as the loan's principal balance is greater than 78% of the original loan amount. This insurance will be removed as soon as the principal owed is less than 78% of the original loan amount and the payments have been made on time for the past five years. FHA loans can be fixed or ARMs depending upon the consumer's choice.

Conventional loans allowed consumers to finance up to 100% of their home's value over the past decade, but those days are long gone as the conventional market reels from the credit crunch and the accompanying housing crises. Currently, conventional loans allow consumers to finance up to 90% of their home's value and this may be limited to 80% soon, as many lenders refuse to offer 2nd mortgages on top of 80% 1st mortgages.

Recently, FHA loans have become more attractive because homeowners and buyers are required to put as little as 3% down to purchase or refinance their homes. FHA loans also allow the 3% to be a gift from a relative, non-profit organization or government agency. Although you will have to pay mortgage insurance (MI), these loans have offered homeowners a way out from their conventional high interest rate ARMs. Consumers will still have to qualify for their loan based on property value, documented income and meet other FHA credit requirements.

Be warned; many consumers believe that because they are choosing an FHA loan that the government is making sure that they will not pay too much for the loan. This could not be further from the truth. Lenders and brokers can charge up-front fees and still earn large rebates by raising your interest rate. As has been said before, the federal government is not looking out for the consumer.

Homeowners who are currently stuck in an ARM loan because their LTV is greater than 90% of their home's value should consider refinancing through the FHA. Consumers must work with a professional loan officer who will give them accurate monthly payment estimates to ensure homeowners are not trading one bad loan for another. Consumers should contact the FHA directly either by email at hud@custhelp.com or call 1 (800) 225-5342 to find out if an FHA loan could assist them in holding onto their home.

Stated Income Loans

Stated income loans are exactly what their name implies. It is also called the "liar" loan. Instead of documenting your income, you state your income, telling the lender what your gross monthly income is, and lenders do not ask for confirmation. Due to the higher risk associated with these loans, borrowers have to pay higher rates for the same loans wage earners are receiving who documented their income. Stated income loans were originally designed for individuals who were self-employed or owned a business. These borrowers have to file a Schedule C (expense write-offs) with their tax return. Since lenders looked at the income after write-offs, many of these borrowers looked like they had very little income. Lenders knew that the self-employed borrower's income fell somewhere between their gross and net income, so they allowed them to state their income, presumably to show their true ability to afford a loan. This type of loan invited inflated income numbers from borrowers, and loan officers were more than willing to coach their borrowers into inflating their gross income. The loan officers didn't care; they were not signing the loan application under penalty of perjury.

The real problems arose when the lending industry began allowing wage earners, those who file W-2s, to state their income instead of documenting it. Most wage earners have set wages, except those who receive monthly bonuses and overtime. There were cases in which janitors were stating that they made $60,000 per year. These grossly inflated numbers allowed low-income borrowers to purchase increasingly costly homes, many of which were beyond the borrower's ability to pay.

> "If you are a W-2'd employee, don't purchase a home using a stated income loan; you probably can't afford the home if you must inflate your income."

If you are a wage earner, don't fall into this trap. Your income must be able to support the loan; and if you must inflate your income to qualify, it is a great indicator that you are buying a home that is beyond your price range. Additionally, there were loans that allowed a borrower to state their assets, called the "Stated Income/Stated Assets" loan. The industry referred to these loans as the "liar, liar" loan. Everyone knew that these numbers were not to be believed and they left many borrowers way over their heads, in loans they could not afford.

Loan to Value (LTV)/Combined Loan of Value (CLTV)

The LTV designates the amount of your loan vs. the value of your home. As an example, if your home is worth $500,000 and your loan is $400,000, your LTV is 80%. The CLTV is used when you take out a second mortgage on your home and is the combined loan amount of your first and second mortgages. For instance, if you took out a second mortgage of $50,000 on the example above, your CLTV would be 90% on your $500,000 home.

The closer the loan amount gets to the value of your home, the greater the risk to the lender and the higher the interest rate you will pay. If your CLTV is less than 70% and you have a good FICO score, generally you will not have to pay any more than the available interest rate given to the most credit-worthy borrowers. This is also why second mortgages have higher interest rates. Not only are you getting closer to the value of your home, but it is more difficult for a second mortgage lender to collect their debt if your home is foreclosed on.

If you are purchasing or refinancing a home that is within the conforming loan limits and does not exceed 80% LTV, you should qualify for the rates based on your FICO and income alone without facing an increase to your interest rate. This is due to Fannie Mae and Freddie Mac guidelines that limit loans to 80% LTV. If you need to take out a 2nd mortgage on your home, not only will the second mortgage rate be higher, but it will affect the rate on your 1st mortgage. You can exceed 80% LTV on your "A" paper 1st mortgage, but if you do you will have to pay PMI (Private Mortgage Insurance) and that can be costly.

Sub-prime lenders will not be as willing to go to the higher LTV's without your interest rate rising dramatically. Many of the sub-prime lenders are no longer in business due to past borrowers defaulting on their loans. This has caused private investors to cease taking the risk that these loans present and the money supply has disappeared. Most sub-prime lenders will limit the LTV to 70%, so that if the borrower defaults they will likely recoup their loss through the sale of the home.

In past years, because of the high appreciation in home values, lenders were willing to give loans that had CLTVs of 100%. Those days are gone and currently the best you can get on the market is a 90% CLTV. There may be some exceptions, but good luck finding them.

Rule #25

"The higher your LTV, the higher the interest rate for your loan."

The value of your home is based on an appraiser's evaluation of your property and includes such factors as sales comparables in your neighborhood that have occurred in the last six months, condition of the home and any upgrades that you have such as granite countertops, wood or tile floors in the kitchen and bathrooms. Many homeowners mistakenly believe that they can look at the asking price of homes in their neighborhood and figure out what their home is worth.

A competent broker should be able to give you a reasonable estimate (though not professional) of the price range your home's value falls within. The broker will also let you know that you can't count on their estimate because there may be many factors that drive the value of your home up or down. We leave it to the professional appraisers.

Purchase/Refinance/Cash-Out Refinance

When purchasing a home, the interest rate that you qualify for is governed by the other factors in this chapter. Sometimes, first-time home buyers must pay a little higher rate, but it is not the rule for the industry. Refinancing your home will not affect the rate unless you are pulling cash-out. If you do not exceed 70% LTV on your home, many lenders will not hit you for an increase to your fees of .125%-.25%. Finding these lenders is the broker's job and it is another reason to find an experienced broker that has many lenders to choose from.

If you took out a 1st and a 2nd mortgage on your home when you purchased it, these are called purchase money mortgages. As your home appreciates in value over the coming years, you can refinance both mortgages into a single mortgage so long as the LTV is not over 80%. This is not considered a cash-out because they were both purchase money mortgages.

Any future refinances that increase your loan amount over the current mortgage will be considered cash-out. If you wish to have your loan costs added to your mortgage, lenders do not consider this cash-out; it is part of the costs of your loan. If your refinance allows you to have a few dollars left in your pocket at the end of the loan process, you may not have to pay the higher fees. Each lender has a maximum amount they allow you to pocket at the end of the loan. This is because the exact cost of your loan is not known, due to the variable fees, until the loan is funded and lenders leave you a little wiggle room so that you're not out of pocket any money to pay for your loan.

Prepayment Penalty

This is the worst of all worlds-prepayment penalties are to be avoided at all costs. These penalties can eat up a good chunk of the equity of your home if you have to sell or refinance during the penalty period. If your lender or broker gives you a choice between a prepay and slightly higher rate, take the higher rate. None of us know what the future holds and if the unexpected happens-loss of employment, job transfer or rates dropping dramatically-and you want to lower your rate, choosing to keep yourself tied to a large mortgage is a grievous mistake.

The good news is that most "A" paper loans do not come with a prepayment penalty. You should insist on this from the very beginning of the loan process. There are unscrupulous loan officers who will add a penalty to make more money on your loan. Sub-prime loans usually have a prepayment penalty, usually for the duration of the fixed period of your loan. For example, if you choose a 2/28 loan there will be a two-year prepay period. If you choose a 3/27, it may be three years in duration. Most prepays are for two or three years, but they may be longer, so make sure you know exactly how long the pre-pay period is before you sign the loan documents. Even sub-prime loans can have the penalty period removed, but be willing to pay an extra .5% to your interest rate.

Rule #26

"If you have good to excellent credit, you should not have a pre-payment penalty; insist on it."

Some loan officers will try to talk you into accepting a penalty, presenting it as a way to save money. They will ask you how long you intend to stay in your home, and most of us think we will be in our homes for at least a couple of years. But remember, if you have good credit this should not be part of your loan.

There are many types of prepayment penalties, but the calculation most often used in the lending industry is very difficult to understand, with the way it is worded in your loan documents. Let me try to simplify it for you. The calculation is as follows: Take your current mortgage balance (what you owe) and multiply it by 80% (.8), then multiply this by the current interest rate (not the teaser rate in an Option ARM) and then divide by 2. This calculation allows the lender to get a great deal of money from you if you decide to leave your loan. In plain English, it is 80% of your loan amount, times your interest rate, for a six-month period.

It doesn't sound like it would be that much, but look at the following tables and you can see how much it would cost you. We will assume a few different loan amounts: in Table 5.1 a current interest rate of 7% and in Table 5.2 a 6% interest rate.

Table 5.1

Mortgage Balance		80%	Interest Rate 7%		Penalty
$200,000	x.8	$160,000	.07	x.5	$5,600
$400,000	x.8	$320,000	.07	x.5	$11,200
$500,000	x.8	$400,000	.07	x.5	$14,000
$750,000	x.8	$600,000	.07	x.5	$21,000
$1,000,000	x.8	$800,000	.07	x.5	$28,000

Table 5.2

Mortgage Balance		80%	Interest Rate 6%		Penalty
$200,000	x.8	$160,000	.06	x.5	$4,800
$400,000	x.8	$320,000	.06	x.5	$9,600
$500,000	x.8	$400,000	.06	x.5	$12,000
$750,000	x.8	$600,000	.06	x.5	$18,000
$1,000,000	x.8	$800,000	.06	x.5	$24,000

As the tables above demonstrate, the penalty will cost a great deal of money. The only saving grace, if you can't avoid the penalty, is that it is currently tax-deductible.

There are two specific types of penalties associated with 1st mortgages, hard prepays and soft prepays. A hard prepay will require you to pay the penalty whether you refinance or sell your home. The soft prepay will only require you to pay if you refinance your home; it allows you to sell your home without incurring the penalty.

Chapter 7

Understanding Your Loan Documents

Anyone who has experienced the mortgage process is always amazed by the amount of paperwork that is involved. Borrowers receive documents from their broker, lender, title and escrow companies. As the loan moves forward the escrow company calls and sets up a signing time, giving you no time to review the documents. Considering the number of documents and fine print involved, it's enough to give any attorney a headache.

Although all the documents are important, it is necessary to focus on the four key documents that show how much you are paying for your loan and the interest rate you received. These are the Good Faith Estimate, Note, Truth in Lending Statement and estimated settlement statement (Est. HUD-1). As mentioned earlier, the GFE is not a legally binding contract, but it is important to be able to understand the information so that you can compare the fees with those found on the estimated HUD-1 you receive just before signing.

The Real Estate Settlement Procedures Act (RESPA) is the federal law that governs how mortgage loans are to be conducted and assigns numbers for certain fees associated with a mortgage loan on the GFE and HUD-1. They were labeled as such so you can compare the fees when it is time for signing. You will also find that there are many more categories of fees on the HUD-1 as opposed to the GFE. This is due to the fact that many of the numbered items on the HUD-1 are not actually part of your loan costs.

Good Faith Estimate (GFE)

Table 7.1

GOOD FAITH ESTIMATE

Applicants:	Application No:
Property Addr:	Date Prepared:
Prepared By:	Loan Program:

The information provided below reflects estimates of the charges which you are likely to incur at the settlement of your loan. The fees listed are estimates–actual charges may be more or less. Your transaction may not involve a fee for every item listed. The numbers listed beside the estimates generally correspond to the numbered lines contained in the HUD-1 settlement statement which you will be receiving at settlement. The HUD-1 settlement statement will show you the actual cost for items paid at settlement.

Total Loan Amount $ Interest Rate: %   Term: mths

800	ITEMS PAYABLE IN CONNECTION WITH LOAN:			PFC S F POC
801	Loan Origination Fee		$	
802	Loan Discount			
803	Appraisal Fee			
804	Credit Report			
805	Lender's Inspection Fee			
808	Mortgage Broker Fee			
809	Tax Related Service Fee			
810	Processing Fee			
811	Underwriting Fee			
812	Wire Transfer Fee			

1100	TITLE CHARGES:			PFC S F POC
1101	Closing or Escrow Fee:		$	
1105	Document Preparation Fee			
1106	Notary Fees			
1107	Attorney Fees			
1108	Title Insurance:			

1200	GOVERNMENT RECORDING & TRANSFER CHARGES:			PFC S F POC
1201	Recording Fees:		$	
1202	City/County Tax/Stamps:			
1203	State Tax/Stamps			

1300	ADDITIONAL SETTLEMENT CHARGES:			PFC S F POC
1302	Pest Inspection		$	

Estimated Closing Costs

900	ITEMS REQUIRED BY LENDER TO BE PAID IN ADVANCE:			PFC S F POC
901	Interest for	days @ $	per day $	
902	Mortgage Insurance Premium			
903	Hazard Insurance Premium			
904				
905	VA Funding Fee			

1000	RESERVES DEPOSITED WITH LENDER:			PFC S F POC
1001	Hazard Insurance Premiums	months @ $	per month $	
1002	Mortgage Ins. Premium Reserves	months @ $	per month	
1003	School Tax	months @ $	per month	
1004	Taxes and Assessment Reserves	months @ $	per month	
1005	Flood Insurance Reserves	months @ $	per month	
		months @ $	per month	
		months @ $	per month	

Estimated Prepaid Items/Reserves

TOTAL ESTIMATED SETTLEMENT CHARGES

TOTAL ESTIMATED FUNDS NEEDED TO CLOSE:		TOTAL ESTIMATED MONTHLY PAYMENT:
Purchase Price/Payoff (+)	New First Mortgage(-)	Principal & Interest
Loan Amount (-)	Sub Financing(-)	Other Financing (P & I)
Est. Closing Costs (+)	New 2nd Mtg Closing Costs(+)	Hazard Insurance
Est. Prepaid Items/Reserves (+)		Real Estate Taxes
Amount Paid by Seller (-)		Mortgage Insurance
		Homeowner Assn. Dues
		Other
Total Est. Funds needed to close		Total Monthly Payment

These estimates are provided pursuant to the Real Estate Settlement Procedures Act of 1974, as amended (RESPA). Additional information can be found in the HUD Special Information Booklet, which is to be provided to you by your mortgage broker or lender, if your application is to purchase residential real property and the lender will take a first lien on the property. The undersigned acknowledges receipt of the booklet "Settlement Costs," and if applicable the Consumer Handbook on ARM Mortgages.

Applicant   Date   Applicant   Date

Calyx Form gfe2 frm 11/01

The GFE (Table 7.1) has columns to the right of the fees that are labeled PFC (Prepaid Finance Charge), F (FHA allowable), S (Seller Paid) and POC (Paid Out of Closing). The columns that are most important are the PFC and POC. Fees that have PFC checked are items that are included in the APR. POC fees are those that have been paid outside of your loan, such as the appraisal fee that has been paid for at the time of the appraisal. Please take note that the sections are not in numbered order, they usually will address broker and lender fees first, then title charges, government recording and transfer charges, additional settlement charges, items required by the lender to be paid in advance, reserves deposited with lender, compensation to broker and total funds needed to close.

Located at the top of the GFE you should see the loan amount, the interest rate and term of your loan. The term will be expressed in months, such as 360/360, which indicates a 30-year amortized loan. This does not indicate how long your fixed period is, so don't take this as confirmation that you are receiving a 30-year fixed loan.

Section 800

Table 7.2

801 Loan Origination Fee	+ $	$	
802 Loan Discount			
803 Appraisal Fee		(350.00)	√
804 Credit Report		22.33	√
805 Lender's Inspection Fee			
808 Mortgage Broker Fee			
809 Tax Related Service Fee			
810 Processing Fee			
811 Underwriting Fee			
812 Wire Transfer Fee			

All of the fees designated 800s will either be prepaid finance charges or paid out of closing. They are one time fees. When choosing an FHA loan, FHA approved fees will have the "F" column marked. If your GFE does not designate the type of fee by checking the appropriate right-hand column, ask your loan officer to place the appropriate check marks in these columns. All of these fees will be prepaid finance charges except the appraisal, and so long as they are labeled as such they will be calculated into the APR. If your loan officer fails to label the PFCs, you will not receive an accurate APR on your Truth in Lending Statement when you request it early in the loan process.

Whether you are working with a broker or lender, most loan officers will place your Points on the Origination Line 801. This will be expressed as a fee, but it is usually a percentage of your loan amount. For example, if you are paying 1 Point on a $400,000 loan, the fee will be $4,000. The broker or lender can also set a specific amount that is not a percentage of your loan, if you negotiate for a fixed fee. When working with a broker, lender fees should be designated items in the 800 section in addition to the broker fees.

Line 802 will designate the discount Points you paid to receive you interest rate. Many loan officers will omit this because they don't want you to know that you received a great rate while having to pay thousands of dollars to get it. They will hide the fee on other lines or omit it entirely, which will affect the accuracy of the APR on the Truth in Lending Statement you will request. Line 803 will show your appraisal fee and should be check marked as a POC cost, when it is paid by the borrower at the time the appraisal is conducted. Line 804 will show your credit inquiry fee and it is a prepaid finance charge, so it should be calculated as part of your APR. Make sure the appropriate check is in the right-hand column. Line 808 is a tax service fee, which can be a junk fee in some circumstances. Line 809 is labeled an underwriting fee and will be charged by the lender, whether you are working with a lender or broker.

Line 814 is where the loan officer should place the Yield Spread Premium (YSP) or rebate that they are charging you. Almost all loans have a YSP, and almost all loan officers fail to identify this fee in the GFE. If there is no YSP indicated, question your loan officer thoroughly about this, because in 9 out of 10 cases, they are hiding the real cost of your loan.

> "If Line 814 (YSP) has no fee listed, odds are you are dealing with a loan officer that is hiding the true cost of your loan. Tell the loan officer that if you find out that they charged you a YSP (whether they are a broker or a lender), without disclosing it; you will cancel your loan and they will have wasted their time. Use the APR calculator to identify the hidden rebate fee before signing your loan documents."

Line 816 will indicate the broker's up-front fee. Brokers will generally place this fee on Line 801 because there should be no Points charged by a lender on Line 801 when a broker is processing your loan. This should also be identified as a 'prepaid finance charge" and be included in your APR calculation. Line 818 is the processing fee charged by lenders and should be included in your APR as a prepaid finance charge.

Section 1100

Table 7.3

1100 Title Charges		PFC S F POC
1101 Closing or Escrow Fee	$	
1105 Document Preparation Fee		
1106 Notary Fee		
1107 Attorney Fee		
1108 Title Insurance		
1112 Title Search		

Title and escrow charges are labeled as 1100s and are not considered "prepaid finance charges" and therefore, not calculated as part of the APR. Item 1101 will show your escrow fee. Line 1105 is the document preparation fee. Line 1106 is the notary fee. When using a mobile notary who comes out to your home, the fee should be approximately $150. In states that require an attorney to handle escrow, line 1107 will indicate the charges. Line 1108 will indicate the fee for your title insurance and line 1112 will show the charge for a title search, which is required by most lenders. Table 7.3 shows the fees included in this section.

Section 1200

The government recording and transfer charges are designated 1200s. This section will show the County recording fees (Line 1201), City/County Tax/Stamps (Line 1202), State Tax or Stamps (Line 1203) as seen in Table 7.4.

Table 7.4

1200 Government Recording and Transfer Charges	PFC S F POC
1201 Recording Fee $	
1202 City/County Tax/Stamps	
1203 State Tax/Stamps	

Section 1300

This section is labeled "Additional Settlement Charges" and contains miscellaneous fees, but there should not be too many of them. There may be a flood survey (Line 1301) and certificate (Line 1305) and possibly a funding fee (Line 1307). Some of these fees are not identified in the GFE (see Table 7.5) because not all states have the same fees and the software used in the industry does not always list all of them. They must be added by the broker or lender prior to giving them to the borrower. In this section, you will find the total estimated closing costs, these are the total up-front fees charged by the broker and lender.

Table 7.5

1300 Additional Settlement Charges	PFC S F POC
1302 Pest Inspection $	
Estimated Closing Costs	

Section 900

The next section is designated "Items Required by Lender to be Paid in Advance." Section 900 indicates items that you will be required to prepay, such as, daily accrued interest, mortgage insurance and hazard insurance premiums. Under RESPA, these fees are not considered PFCs, so they are not calculated into your APR. Line 901 will indicate the daily interest from the closing of your loan until the end of the month. Line 902 will show the mortgage insurance (MI), if you elected to pay MI as opposed to taking a 2nd mortgage on your home. Line 904 will show a flood insurance premium, when the property is in a flood zone. Table 7.6 shows this section of the GFE.

Table 7.6

900 Items Required by Lender to be Paid in Advance			PFC S F POC
901 Interest for days@ $ per day		$	
902 Mortgage Insurance Premium			
903 Hazard Insurance Premium			
904			
905 VA Funding Fee			

Section 1000

Section 1000 is labeled "Reserves Deposited with Lender" and is not part of the APR. This section is used, if you elect to have an escrow account that includes your property taxes and homeowner's insurance added to your monthly mortgage payment and is shown in Table 7.7. Line 1001 will show the hazard insurance deposited and Line 1002 will have the MI that is required in advance. Line 1004 will indicate the amount of monthly taxes that will be held in reserve by the lender. Line 1006 will show the flood insurance if you have to purchase this type of coverage. At the bottom of this section, you will find the total estimated settlement charges; this is the total costs of your loan.

Table 7.7

1000 Reserves Deposited with Lender		PFC S F POC
1001 Hazard Insurance Premium	months@	per month $
1002 Mortgage Ins. Premium	months@	per month
1003 School Tax	months@	per month

1004 Taxes and Assessment	months@	per month
1005 Flood Insurance Reserves	months@	per month
	months@	per month
	months@	per month
Estimated Prepaid Items/Reserves $		
Total Estimated Settlement Charges		$

Loan Totals & Monthly Payment

The final section of the GFE has three parts, one that indicates the total loan amount, closing costs, estimated prepaid items and costs of a 2nd mortgage if applicable. Any rebate received by the broker should be identified in this section, but many brokers do not bother informing their clients of the hidden costs of the loan. These totals are shown in Table 7.8. The second section will show you the monthly payment on your mortgage, hazard insurance, property taxes and any other recurring costs after your loan is closed. The recurring costs are shown in Table 7.9. It is important for all borrowers to understand that the total monthly payment includes all monthly payments, whether or not you choose to have an escrow account and will indicate whether you can afford the home you are purchasing or refinancing.

Table 7.8

Compensation To Broker (Not Paid Out of Loan Proceeds) $	
Total Estimated Funds Needed to Close	
Purchase Price/Payoff (+)	New First Mortgage
Loan Amount (-)	Sub-Financing
Est. Closing Cost (+)	New 2nd Mortgage Cost
Est. Prepaid Items/Reserves (+)	
Amount Paid by Seller (-)	
Total Est. Funds to you	

Table 7.9

	Total Estimated Monthly Payment
	Principal and Interest $
	Other Financing P & I
	Hazard Insurance
	Real Estate Taxes
	Mortgage Insurance
	Homeowner's Assoc. Dues
	Other
	Total Monthly Payment

Promissory Note

The Promissory Note is one of the most important documents and the easiest to understand. This is the contractual agreement that you are entering into with your lending. It will contain the property address, the lender's name, the amount financed, maturity date of the loan and the interest that will accrue. The Note will have the interest rate that you are promising to pay, hopefully the one that you agreed to at the beginning of the loan process. Few loan officers try to change the interest rate because it is so obvious and they would much rather hide fees in the APR than alarm you with a higher interest rate, thereby endangering their loan.

It is still a good idea to watch out for a change in the rate because there are some loan officers that gamble on interest rates coming down during the following weeks. They can increase their rebate if their gamble pays off, but if they were wrong and the interest rate increases they will try to pass the higher rate on to you and it will cost you thousands in extra interest payments throughout the life of your loan.

If the interest rate is not what you were promised, have it corrected prior to signing. Don't believe the loan officer when he or she tells you they will change it later, once you sign, you are accepting that rate. It may indicate there is a prepayment penalty, but not all of them do on their face. Ask you escrow agent if there are any addendums to the Note which may contain further informa-tion, such as the prepayment penalty. An example of a Promissory Note can be found in Table 7.10.

Table 7.10

<table>
<tr><td colspan="3" align="center">**Note**</td></tr>
<tr><td>[Date]</td><td align="center">[City]</td><td align="right">[State]</td></tr>
</table>

[Property Address]

1. BORROWER'S PROMISE TO PAY
In return for a loan that I have received, I promise to pay U.S. $**[Loan Amount]** (this is called "Principal"), plus interest, to the order of the Lender. The Lender is [Lender's Name], a bank which is organized and existing under the laws of the United States of America. I will make all payments under this Note in the form of cash, check or money order.

I understand that the Lender may transfer the Note. The Lender or anyone who takes this Note by transfer and who is entitled to receive payments under this Note is called the "Note Holder."

2. INTEREST
Interest will be charged on unpaid Principal until the full amount of Principal has been paid. I will pay interest at a yearly rate of [**THE ACTUAL INTEREST RATE WILL BE PLACED HERE**] %. The interest rate required by this Section 2 is the rate I will pay both before and after any default described in Section 6(B) of this Note.

3. PAYMENTS
(A) **Time and Place of Payment**
I will pay principal and interest by make a payment every month.

I will make my monthly payment on the [First] day of each month begin-ning on [Date First Payment is Due]. I will make these payments every month until I have paid all of the principal and interest and any other charges described below that I may owe under this Note. Each monthly payment will be applied as of its scheduled due date and will be applied to interest before Principal. If, on [**Last Payment Date**], I still owe amounts under this Note, I will pay those amounts in full on that date, which is call the "Maturity Date."

I will make my monthly payments at [Name and Address of Current Note Holder]

(B) Amount of Monthly Payment

My monthly payment will be in the amount of U.S. $[THE MONTHLY PAYMENT WILL BE PLACED HERE].

4. BORROWER'S RIGHT TO PREPAY [In this example there is "No" Penalty]

I have the right to make payments of Principal at any time before they are due. A payment of Principal only is known as a "Prepayment." When I make a Prepayment, I will tell the Note Holder in writing, that I am doing so. I may not designate a payment as a Prepayment if I have not made all the monthly payments due under the Note.

I may make a full Prepayment or partial Prepayment without paying a Prepayment charge. The Note Holder will use my Prepayments to reduce the amount of Principal that I owe under this Note. However, the Note Holder may apply my Prepayment to the accrued and unpaid interest on the Prepayment amount, before applying my Prepayment to reduce the Principal amount of the Note. If I make a partial Prepayment, there will be no changes in the due date or in the amount of my monthly payments unless the Note Holder agrees in writing to those changes.

Truth in Lending Statement

The Truth in Lending Statement is critical in determining how much your loan is costing you and the terms of your loan. Although it is not a legally binding contract, failure to disclose this information may give a borrower the right to rescind the loan and recover the costs of the loan. It seems at first to be a difficult task for many to understand, due to all the numbers strewn throughout the page, but after a short explanation you will be able to read this document without great effort. The Truth in Lending Statement is a legal size document, and as such, we have split the page with the top half shown in Table 7.11 and bottom half in Table 7.12.

Table 7.11

TRUTH-IN-LENDING DISCLOSURE STATEMENT			
(THIS IS NEITHER A CONTRACT NOR A COMMITMENT TO LEND)			

Applicants: Prepared By:

Property Address:

Application No: Date Prepared:

ANNUAL PERCENTAGE RATE	FINANCE CHARGE	AMOUNT FINANCED	TOTAL OF PAYMENTS
The cost of your credit as a yearly rate	The dollar amount the credit will cost you	The amount of credit provided to you or on your behalf	The amount you will have paid after making all payments as scheduled
%	$	$	$

☐ REQUIRED DEPOSIT: The annual percentage rate does not take into account your required deposit
PAYMENTS: Your payment schedule will be:

Number of Payments	Amount of Payments **	When Payments Are Due	Number of Payments	Amount of Payments **	When Payments Are Due	Number of Payments	Amount of Payments **	When Payments Are Due

☐ DEMAND FEATURE: This obligation has a demand feature.
☐ VARIABLE RATE FEATURE: This loan contains a variable rate feature. A variable rate disclosure has been provided earlier.

Courtesy of Calyx Software

Contained in this document is your APR, the most important indicator of how much your loan cost. Following the instructions in Chapter 8, you will already have been given your Truth in Lending Statement long before your signing date and will have used the APR calculator on the website that I referred you to, so you will know exactly how much your lender or broker is charging you. Make sure the APR that you were promised is the same as that found on the Truth in Lending Statement received at signing. Sometimes there are errors that occur within the documents and these can be fixed in a short period of time.

Your statement will also include the finance charge, the cost of borrowing the money for your home. This number has a tendency to scare many borrowers because it is usually a larger number than the amount originally borrowed. To simplify this, if you are paying 6% on $100,000 over 30 years, your yearly interest will be $6,000 at the beginning of your loan, although it does shrink as the principal owed diminishes, multiplying $6,000 x 30 (Years) = $180,000 in interest. Again, this is not an accurate calculation, but you can see how the interest adds up.

The next section to look at is the payment schedule. A 30-year fixed loan will show only two payments; the monthly payment you were promised for 359 months, and one payment that is slightly different, which is your last payment on month 360 as shown in the following payment schedule.

Number of Payments	Amount of Payments	When Payments Are Due
359	$2,240.00	07/01/2008
1	$2,242.00	06/01/2037

An adjustable-rate mortgage such as a 5/1 ARM would have three different payments shown; the fixed period for 60 months, adjustable payment for 299 months and the last payment that is always a few dollars different than the other payments. The monthly payment amount is based on the current index rate and margin, but this is only an estimate, as the index will have changed by the time your fixed period ends. During periods when indexes are low, this payment can be extremely misleading. The payment for the 299 months is by no means set in stone. The following is an example of a 5/1 ARM payment schedule.

Number of Payments	Amount of Payments	When Payments Are Due
60	$2,240.00	07/01/2008
299	$2,420.00	07/01/2013
1	$2,428.00	06/01/2037

The payment schedules for Option ARM loans are much more complicated, so if you see that your payment schedule has numerous pay periods, question your loan officer. The trap that so many borrowers fall into is that they see the teaser rate payment for a specific period, such as, five years and the payments look incredibly low. Remember, unless you want to face huge monthly payments in as little as a few months, don't rely on the monthly payment presented on the Truth in Lending statement for the Option ARM loan.

When taking out a 2nd mortgage, whether fixed or an equity line, you will notice that there are two payment amounts. The first is the monthly payment for 15 years and the second is the balloon payment that is due at the end of the 15th year. Most second mortgages are amortized over 30 years, but due in 15. The following is an example of what a $100,000 fixed 2ⁿᵈ payment schedule might look like.

Number of Payments	Amount of Payments	When Payments Are Due
179	$599.55	07/01/2008
1	$71,648.52	06/01/2023

In addition, the "Demand Feature" box would be checked, because the balloon payment is considered a demand that you pay the remaining balance at the end of the 15ᵗʰ year. Below the payment schedule section are two boxes the "Demand Feature" as just mentioned, and the "Variable Rate Feature" box. If the variable box has been checked, your loan has some variable feature to it. You can look above in the payment schedule section to see how long the fixed period is as described above.

> "If you requested a 30-year fixed loan, and the 'Variable Rate Feature' box has been checked; you're not getting what you were promised."

The bottom half of the Truth in Lending Statement has multiple boxes that may be checked depending upon the loan terms, as seen in Table 7.4. All lenders will require you to have homeowner's insurance, so this box will be checked. When the property is in a flood zone, you may be required to purchase flood insurance. There is a section that addresses whether or not you have a prepayment penalty with your loan. There is only one of two choices that will be indicated, "You may have a prepayment penalty" or "You will not have a prepayment penalty." If you agreed to a penalty, the "may" box will be checked and you need to look at the prepayment clause in the Note to confirm it is for term you agreed. Loans with no prepayment penalty will have the box stating you "will not" have a penalty will be checked.

Table 7.12

CREDIT LIFE/CREDIT DISABILITY: Credit life insurance and credit disability insurance are not required to obtain credit, and will not be provided unless you sign and agree to pay the additional cost.			
Type	Premium	Signature	
Credit Life		I want credit life insurance.	Signature:
Credit Disability		I want credit disability insurance.	Signature:
Credit Life and Disability		I want credit life and disability insurance.	Signature:

INSURANCE: The following insurance is required to obtain credit:
☐ Credit life insurance ☐ Credit disability ☐ Property insurance ☐ Flood insurance
You may obtain the insurance from anyone you want that is acceptable to creditor
☐ If you purchase ☐ property ☐ flood insurance from creditor you will pay $ for a one year term.
SECURITY: You are giving a security interest in:
☐ The goods or property being purchased   ☐ Real property you already own.
FILING FEES: $
LATE CHARGE: If a payment is more than   days late, you will be charged   %
PREPAYMENT: If you pay off early, you
☐ may   ☐ will not   have to pay a penalty.
☐ may   ☐ will not   be entitled to a refund of part of the finance charge.
ASSUMPTION: Someone buying your property
☐ may   ☐ may, subject to conditions   ☐ may not   assume the remainder of your loan on the original terms.
See your contract documents for any additional information about nonpayment, default, any required repayment in full before the scheduled date and prepayment refunds and penalties
☐ * means an estimate   ☐ all dates and numerical disclosures except the late payment disclosures are estimates.

* * NOTE: The Payments shown above include reserve deposits for Mortgage Insurance (if applicable), but exclude Property Taxes and Insurance.

THE UNDERSIGNED ACKNOWLEDGES RECEIVING A COMPLETED COPY OF THIS DISCLOSURE.

_____   _____
(Applicant)   (Date)   (Applicant)   (Date)

Courtesy of Calyx Software

Rule #27

"If the Truth in Lending Statement says 'You may have a prepayment penalty;' you do."

When the Truth in Lending Statement states, "You may have a Pre-payment Penalty," you do, the only question is; how long is the penalty period? Don't let your loan officer tell you that it means that they might charge you a penalty, but won't. A loan with no prepayment penalty will NEVER have the "may" box checked. I have heard all kinds of excuses why the "may" box was checked. It is not the loan officer's word that is taken when you try to refinance or sell your home in a year or two; it is what you agreed to in the Note, but unless the loan officer is exceptionally deceptive, the Truth in Lending Statement will have the appropriate box checked. Be very careful and do not sign your loan documents, if they try to surprise you with a penalty. As shown in Chapter 5, it can be very costly.

Lenders may allow for the assumption of your loan by another person, so the box "may, subject to conditions" assume the remainder of your loan on the original terms, will be checked. The new borrower will have to qualify for the loan and if they can not the lender will not agree to them assuming the current mortgage.

Settlement Statement (HUD-1)

The estimated HUD-1 is the document that you will receive prior to or on the date of signing. It is only an estimate, because the date on which your loan funds will determine a few of the fees, as discussed earlier. The estimated HUD-1 should be a very close representation of the final fees that you will incur. The categories that identify the fees and other items are governed by RESPA. You will notice that there are additional items that were not found on your GFE. These categories are not part of your fee structure.

The HUD-1 will indicate the type of loan, borrower, loan number, lender and escrow agent. A purchase will also indicate the seller's name and address. All settlement statements have two columns; one for borrower's information and the other for the seller's information. If you are refinancing the seller's information will be blank, since no seller is involved in the transaction.

The first page indicates the purchase contract price, settlement charges (pay-offs, such as credit cards, etc.) and existing loan payoff amount. The "Gross Amount Due From Borrower" is the total amount needed to either purchase or refinance your home. When purchasing a home, Line 301 will include the purchase price of the home and all fees charged for your loan. Sometimes the seller will give a credit to buyers and this will be included on Page 1 in section 200. If refinancing, Line 301 shows the gross amount due from the borrower; this is the total of the prior loan payoff amount, loan costs and any debts that you are paying off. If you decided to receive some cash-out when refinancing Line 303 will indicate cash to the borrower. Line 303 will also indicate if you owe money, for instance, if you decided to pay out-of-pocket for your loan. The sections that are numbered 100-219 have no bearing on the costs of the loan.

Table 7.13

A.	U.S. DEPARTMENT OF HOUSING AND URBAN DEVELOPMENT	SETTLEMENT STATEMENT

B. TYPE OF LOAN	1. ☐ FHA	2. ☐ FmHA	6. File Number	7. Loan Number
3. ☐ CONV. UNINS.	4. ☐ VA	5. ☐ CONV. INS.	8. Mortgage Insurance Case Number	

C. NOTE: This form is furnished to give you a statement of actual settlement costs. Amounts paid to and by the settlement agent are shown. Items marked "(p.o.c.)" were paid outside the closing; they are shown here for informational purposes and are not included in the totals.

D. NAME AND ADDRESS OF BORROWER:	E. NAME AND ADDRESS OF SELLER:	F. NAME AND ADDRESS OF LENDER:
G. PROPERTY LOCATION:	H. SETTLEMENT AGENT: NAME, AND ADDRESS	
	PLACE OF SETTLEMENT:	I. SETTLEMENT DATE:

J. SUMMARY OF BORROWER'S TRANSACTION		K. SUMMARY OF SELLER'S TRANSACTION	
100. GROSS AMOUNT DUE FROM BORROWER:		**400. GROSS AMOUNT DUE TO SELLER:**	
101. Contract sales price		401. Contract sales price	
102. Personal property		402. Personal property	
103. Settlement charges to borrower (line 1400)		403.	
104.		404.	
105.		405.	
Adjustments for items paid by seller in advance		*Adjustments for items paid by seller in advance*	
106. City/town taxes to		406. City/town taxes to	
107. County taxes to		407. County taxes to	
108. Assessments to		408. Assessments to	
109.		409.	
110.		410.	
111.		411.	
112.		412.	
120. GROSS AMOUNT DUE FROM BORROWER		**420. GROSS AMOUNT DUE TO SELLER**	
200. AMOUNTS PAID BY OR IN BEHALF OF BORROWER:		**500. REDUCTIONS IN AMOUNT DUE TO SELLER:**	
201. Deposit of earnest money		501. Excess deposit (see instructions)	
202. Principal amount of new loan(s)		502. Settlement charges to seller (line 1400)	
203. Existing loan(s) taken subject to		503. Existing loan(s) taken subject to	
204.		504. Payoff of first mortgage loan	
205.		505. Payoff of second mortgage loan	
206.		506.	
207.		507.	
208.		508.	
209.		509.	
Adjustments for items unpaid by seller		*Adjustments for items unpaid by seller*	
210. City/town taxes to		510. City/town taxes to	
211. County taxes to		511. County taxes to	
212. Assessments to		512. Assessments to	
213.		513.	
214.		514.	
215.		515.	
216.		516.	
217.		517.	
218.		518.	
219.		519.	
220. TOTAL PAID BY/FOR BORROWER		**520. TOTAL REDUCTION AMOUNT DUE SELLER**	
300. CASH AT SETTLEMENT FROM/TO BORROWER		**600. CASH AT SETTLEMENT TO/FROM SELLER**	
301. Gross amount due from borrower (line 120)		601. Gross amount due to seller (line 420)	
302. Less amounts paid by/for borrower (line 220)		602. Less reductions in amount due seller (line 520)	
303. CASH (☐ FROM) (☐ TO) BORROWER		**603. CASH (☐ TO) (☐ FROM) SELLER**	

Courtesy copy from HUD "Buying Your Home–Settlement Costs and Useful Information" HUD-398-H(4) June '97

The second page of the estimated HUD-1 (Table 7.15) should look familiar; all of these fees were included in your GFE and have been discussed above. Sections 800, 900, 1000, 1100, 1200 and 1300 are all sections of the GFE. **This page should be compared to the GFE fees to ensure your broker or lender is not adding any significant charges that were not included at the beginning of the loan process.** I will not describe them line by line, because you can refer to the GFE section of this chapter to understand each of the fees and compare the estimated costs with those actually being charged.

It is important to review section 800 carefully, if you are working with a broker. Not only will their origination fee be contained in this section, but if a broker receives a YSP, it will be stated in this section. Remember, the YSP is not a fee that you pay, so it will only be identified on the description line and have the dollar amount in that area, labeled as a "Paid Out of Closing" (POC) fee. Also, if you are working with a lender, correspondent broker or a broker with a warehouse line, you will not see any fee mentioned on the estimated HUD-1, since current law does not require them to disclose the rebates they receive. Brokers that are required by law to disclose the YSP will do so on line 808.

Table 7.14

	Paid from Borrower's Funds at Settlement
806 Mortgage Insurance Application Fee to	$150.00
807 Assumption Fee to	
808 YSP to (your broker's name) $3,500 POC	
809 Origination Fee to (your broker's name)	$4,000.00

Notice that all the other fees are listed under the "Paid from Borrower's Funds at Settlement" column. If you were not reviewing your estimated HUD-1 carefully, you may not catch that there is another fee your broker receives from the lender (for increasing your interest rate). It is plain to see that not only do lenders and brokers wish to keep the YSP hidden from you, but escrow companies will assist indirectly, by hiding the fee on a line where you may not notice it. This isn't the escrow agents fault, Federal law states that the YSP is "Paid Out of Closing" (POC) and is not to be placed in the borrower's cost column. This reminds me of the old saying, "I'm from the government and I'm here to help," thanks a lot.

Table 7.15

L. SETTLEMENT CHARGES			PAID FROM BORROWER'S FUNDS AT SETTLEMENT	PAID FROM SELLER'S FUNDS AT SETTLEMENT
700. TOTAL SALES/BROKER'S COMMISSION based on price $ @ %=				
Division of Commission (line 700) as follows:				
701. $ to				
702. $ to				
703. Commission paid at Settlement				
704.				
800. ITEMS PAYABLE IN CONNECTION WITH LOAN				
801. Loan Origination Fee %				
802. Loan Discount %				
803. Appraisal Fee to				
804. Credit Report to				
805. Lender's Inspection Fee				
806. Mortgage Insurance Application Fee to				
807. Assumption Fee				
808.				
809.				
810.				
811.				
900. ITEMS REQUIRED BY LENDER TO BE PAID IN ADVANCE				
901. Interest from to @$ /day				
902. Mortgage Insurance Premium for months to				
903. Hazard Insurance Premium for years to				
904. years to				
905.				
1000. RESERVES DEPOSITED WITH LENDER				
1001. Hazard Insurance months @ $ per month				
1002. Mortgage Insurance months @ $ per month				
1003. City property taxes months @ $ per month				
1004. County property taxes months @ $ per month				
1005. Annual assessments months @ $ per month				
1006. months @ $ per month				
1007. months @ $ per month				
1008. Aggregate Adjustment months @ $ per month				
1100. TITLE CHARGES				
1101. Settlement or closing fee to				
1102. Abstract or title search to				
1103. Title examination to				
1104. Title insurance binder to				
1105. Document preparation to				
1106. Notary fees to				
1107. Attorney's fees to				
(includes above items numbers:				
1108. Title Insurance to				
(includes above items numbers;				
1109. Lender's coverage $				
1110. Owner's coverage $				
1111.				
1112.				
1113.				
1200. GOVERNMENT RECORDING AND TRANSFER CHARGES				
1201. Recording fees: Deed $; Mortgage $; Releases $				
1202. City/county tax/stamps: Deed $; Mortgage $				
1203. State tax/stamps: Deed $; Mortgage $				
1204.				
1205.				
1300. ADDITIONAL SETTLEMENT CHARGES				
1301. Survey to				
1302. Pest inspection to				
1303.				
1304.				
1305.				
1400. TOTAL SETTLEMENT CHARGES (enter on lines 103, Section J and 502, Section K)				

Courtesy copy from HUD "Buying Your Home–Settlement Costs and Useful Information" HUD-398-H(4) June '97

Section 1300 will show any debts that you are paying off with the loan, such as credit cards, car loans, etc. There may be additional fees which will be located on a supplemental page. Add all the fixed fees together and make sure they match the fee estimates on the original GFE given to you at the start of the loan process.

Generally speaking, your lender or broker should be within $200 of the original estimate (don't expect perfection) regarding all fixed fees. The only fees that will vary are those in sections 900, 1000 and 1100, for the reasons stated in the GFE discussion. If the fixed fees increase dramatically, this is the time to call your loan officer and request a broker or lender credit before signing (get it in writing). Consider moving to a new broker or lender if you can't get a credit.

You must also weigh the added time it will take to begin the loan process again with a new lender or broker. It can save you thousands in fees and interest, but a small savings may not be worth the additional effort. Deciding to stop working with a loan officer mid-way through the process is a difficult decision. Loan officers who routinely raise the fees at the time of signing know consumers don't want to start over again. The mortgage industry will not change its' disreputable practices unless consumers begin to hold them accountable. There are four challenges faced when withdrawing from a loan that is already locked and a few weeks have passed, but a loan that is costing you much more than the fees you were promised may make it worth the trouble.

Finding the extra fees or higher interest rate unacceptable, a consumer faces the possibility that interest rates have increased since they locked their rate with the prior loan officer. This is the greatest financial danger of beginning the process with a new lender or broker. Before making the decision to fire your prior loan officer, visit www.mortgage-maze.net and check today's par rate. You may find out that interest rates are lower than the lock rate you had with the previous lender.

A lower rate is a financial bonanza and a great bargaining chip to deal with the loan officer that has raised your fees. Tell him you will find a new lender or broker if they don't honor the GFE fees. All the pressure will be on them because they have invested a lot of time into your loan; they don't want to lose you. They will know the current interest rates, so don't try to bluff, it won't work.

You have digested a lot of information in the last seven chapters and now it is time to put it to work for you. The next chapter will help you find an honest broker or lender, and will outline the questions to ask and commitments to demand to ensure you are working with an honest lender or broker.

Chapter 8

Finding an Honest Broker or Lender and Working with Them

For everyone who skipped the preceding chapters-I caught you. This chapter will not be very helpful if you have not familiarized yourself with all of the information in the prior chapters.

It's time to get down to searching for an honest loan officer (not necessarily the cheapest). This chapter will show you how to question your loan officer to ensure you are working with a professional and reduce the likelihood that you will have a bad experience. Finding a lender or broker who is totally up-front with all matters regarding your loan is a daunting task. It is not, however, impossible.

Referral from Family or Friends

Many borrowers rely on family, friends, church members and co-workers to refer them to a good broker or lender. This is a good place to start, but do they really know if they got a good deal on their loan? It is doubtful. The truth of the matter is that you will not be one hundred percent sure your loan officer is being truthful with you until the loan documents arrive for signing. By asking the right questions at the start and requesting that all commitments be in writing, you can weed out many of the unscrupulous loan officers.

Comparing Rates

If you are shopping for a loan, you must compare rates on the same day. If you call a broker on Tuesday and then a lender on Wednesday, you are comparing apples and oranges. Rates change daily, sometimes multiple times in one day, and you must invest one day to call at least five different lenders and brokers. You will be in a better position to negotiate, if you already know the best rates available on the day you are looking for a loan. Many industry insiders will tell you that shopping for a loan is a waste of time, but if you know what you are doing, it will take a few phone calls to find a loan officer willing to adhere to the commitments you request.

Rule #28

"If one loan officer quotes rates and fees far lower than everyone else beware; we all get our money from the same place."

Interviewing Your Loan Officer

Your initial conversation with the loan officer will set the tone for all future communications. It is up to you to control the discussion. Don't allow them to divert you from the following interviewing strategy which focuses on their professional experience and intention to keep their promises to you. Let's get started:

1. Ask how long the loan officer has been in the mortgage business. If it is less than two years, think about finding a more experienced individual.

2. Inquire if they have their broker or sales license; many loan officers work for corporations and they are not required to have an individual license. Do you really want to work with someone who hasn't taken the time to educate themselves and pass your state's minimum educational requirements for a sales license?

Working with a licensed loan officer doesn't guarantee they will look out for your best interest, but they do take their profession seriously. If your loan officer is a broker, he or she has been in the mortgage business for at least two years with a sales license (most states require two years' sales experience prior to applying for a broker license).

3. Ask them what the par rate is today?

Be ready for a long period of silence. Many loan officers have never been ask this question and you will immediately let them know you are aware of how they make their fees without disclosing the information.

Don't let them talk about the rate that they are willing to offer you. Visit our website at www.mortgage-maze.net to see today's par rate. If their rate is much lower than today's par rate, they have most likely built in discount Points to make their rate sound lower than everyone else's, but you will be paying for this lower rate with fees built into the loan. If the rate they quote you is .25% above the par rate or more, they are attempting to make more money on your loan in the form of a rebate without telling you about it. Remember: .25% over the par rate will net your loan officer an extra Point (1%) on your loan and you will be paying for it with a higher interest rate over the life of your loan.

4. Since you have obtained all three of your credit reports with scores as advised in Chapter 3, let the loan officer know that you will not give him your Social Security number until he discusses your loan based on your mid-FICO score that you have in hand. Remember, if you have some bad marks on your credit tell them about it up-front. You don't want to waste your time or theirs.

If they don't want to discuss details with you, thank them for their time and move on. I will spend a half hour discussing a loan with a prospective client without requesting their Social Security number, it's part of our business.

Rule #29

"If they won't talk about your loan without getting your Social Security number, find another broker or lender."

5. Ask if they believe today is a good day to lock your rate (9 out of 10 will say yes). This may be true, but ask them the basis of their belief. If they just say

rates are going up, ask what economic indicators are coming out this week that would cause them to rise. You can visit the NASDAQ website at http://www. nasdaq.com/asp/EconodayFrame.asp. This will give you the economic reports that are due out in the next few days and weeks. If they can't answer this question find another loan officer, this one is not a professional and does not take the time to understand the market.

No one can predict with absolute certainty where rates will go from one day to another; but a loan officer who recommends floating (not locking) for a day or two may demonstrate that they have your interests in mind and not their bank account. Also, if you float your rate, it is not set in stone, so the rate and the APR will change accordingly.

6. Ask if they work with any realtors, and if so, how many? This doesn't indicate that they will be honest, but if they work with a few realtors, they may be in the habit of keeping their word. Many professional realtors will drop a dishonest broker quickly, unless of course the realtor is also dishonest. Follow up by asking for the contact information of the realtors they work with. If they answered yes to the question above and can't give you contact information, you know you're speaking with a dishonest loan officer. Make sure you get the office phone number, dishonest loan officers will go to great lengths to deceive you, including giving the cell phone number of the guy in the cubical next to them. Call the realtor the next day and ask about the loan officer's professionalism and how they treat the realtor's clients.

7. If you have seen or heard their advertised rate and APR, ask them what the total fees are, both origination and YSP. If they refuse to answer or give you some reason why they can't, move on to another broker or lender.

> Reasons given for not disclosing the total fees built into the APR that are dishonest:
>
> a. "I don't know what the title and escrow fees are." Title and escrow fees are not pre-paid finance charges and are not part of your APR.
>
> b. "I don't know if you qualify for this loan." Tell the loan officer that you have given them all the relevant information (FICO score, home value & monthly income) and if you're wrong, you understand that it may affect the rate and APR, but this is no reason for them to withhold a fee

estimate, the fees shouldn't change no matter which loan program you qualify for.

c. "I don't know your exact FICO score and it will affect the rate and APR." Again, tell the loan officer you have your FICO scores and that if they are actually lower, you understand that it may change the rate, but insist on the fee estimate.

Commitments to Request

Tell the loan officer you expect certain commitments in advance and if they follow through with their commitments, you will follow through with completing your loan with them. If they are not willing to make these commitments in writing at the outset, find another lender or broker. The commitments to request are as follows:

1. A good faith estimate is to be emailed following the discussion. Federal law requires that you receive a GFE within three days of submitting your loan application. It must include the origination, escrow, title fees and daily interest estimate. Tell them you want no surprises. Some states have additional documents that should be provided, so check with your state's Department of Real Estate.

2. Insist that they keep to the GFE fee estimate. If the numbers change they must eat any fees that were not listed or increased at the time of signing. Get them to email you the commitment so you have it in writing. This applies to fixed fees only.

3. When the loan is locked, request that they email or fax you a copy of the Lock Confirmation (this will show you your rate and YSP). All brokers receive a Lock Confirmation within 48 hours of locking your loan. Direct lenders may not be so willing to give you this, but stay firm and if they want the loan they will give you what you want. Tell them it must show the lock rate and the YSP. If working with a broker, do not accept something on their letterhead, make sure it is from the lender.

4. The rate will not change-at the time of signing. By the time you lock your loan, they will already have your credit scores, so the rate will not

change so long as you did not inaccurately estimated your home's value or monthly income.

5. They will not make more than 1 Point on your loan, origination fees and rebate combined. If the loan is small (under $300,000) expect to pay a little more since all loans require the same amount of work. This is the time to let them know that you will check the rate and APR to ensure they are keeping to the agreed upon fee. Go to www.mortgage-maze.net and use the APR calculator to find out the total fees you are paying.

6. Request a Truth in Lending Statement within 48 hours of locking your loan and the APR that is stated on the Truth in Lending will not increase at the time of signing or you will refuse to sign.

7. If the interest rate changes or the fees increase after the appraisal has been completed, they will allow the appraiser to sign over the appraisal to your new broker. Get this in writing before beginning the loan process. If you are working with a local broker, you can bring the written assurance into small claims court and get your appraisal fee if they refuse to honor the commitment.

8. Confirm they will follow through with all of these commitments without you having to remind them. If he or she says "yes", ask them what they were. This will ensure they are not just giving you lip service.

These commitments will start the loan process on the correct footing. It will also let your loan officer know that you are the one that must be pleased with the experience, not them. Tell them in no uncertain terms that if the fees, rate or APR increase at the time of signing they will lose your business and will have wasted their time. I only say their time because most of them don't care about yours.

During your search for a great loan, you will find that a large number of loan officers will tell you that they can't follow your requests. They will come up with a myriad of reasons, but the truth is that they are not used to disclosing all the relevant information about their loans at the beginning of the process. To find a full disclosure broker in your state, you can visit www.mortgage-maze. net to speak with a broker who will honor all of these commitments and you will have a great experience working with them.

Remember, all broker fees are negotiable. They cannot lower the lender, title and escrow fees because they are not within the control of your broker. Lenders will not be as flexible as a broker, since most of them are large institutions that have set fees and allow their loan officers no room for fee reductions. Many brokers and lenders will inflate the title and escrow fees, only to lower them later and inflate their own fees, so the total cost of your loan remains the same. Don't let them get away with this.

A lender or broker's loan officer will receive 35%, on average, of the total fees from your loan. Generally, lenders will not give their loan officers the ability to reduce your fees. On the other hand, if you are working with a broker, you may find great latitude in their ability to lower their fees. Don't work with a loan officer at a broker's office. Instead, request to work with the named broker, because the loan officers will receive the same small percentage as if you were working with a direct lender. It is easy to see why large lenders and brokers charge so much for their loans, they have to divide up the spoils with their loan officers.

Working with Your Loan Officer

When you feel comfortable with your loan officer, the next step is to let them pull your credit report (Tri-merge report will have all 3 scores and histories in one document).

1. After they review your credit (this can be done in seconds) confirm that the score reflects the mid-FICO you gave them. If it does, tell them you expect the rate and fees to remain the same (your home's value and your income must support the loan). If the FICO score is different, ask them to email you a copy of the credit report, so you can see the scores; don't take their word for it. If they won't send you the report, question whether you want to work with someone who isn't willing to work with you. There is no law prohibiting them from giving you their tri-merge report (all three bureau reports combined into one).

2. Don't work with any loan officer who tries to move you to an Option ARM loan, because they do not have your interests as a high priority. This loan can cost you dearly.

3. Let them make suggestions, as that's part of their job; but don't let them take control of the process or steer you into a loan you didn't want in the first place.

If Your Fees or Rate Has Changed

Most lenders and brokers will not spring added fees on you until the day of your signing. This is why it is very important to ask for all the key documents discussed in Chapter 7 be forwarded to you a day or two before you sign. There will be the obvious fee increases that many in the industry tell you weren't within their control. The truth is that they knew they were going to disregard their promises from the very start. Make sure you check the interest rate on the Note to ensure you are getting the rate you were promised.

Prior to signing your loan officer should have given you the Truth in Lending Statement that contains the APR. After you have agreed on a fee for your loan, you can check if the APR reflects the agreed to lender and broker fees. When you receive the Truth in Lending Statement go to the following website <u>www.mortgage-maze.net</u>-and start performing the calculation described in Chapter 5. If the APR demonstrates they are making more than the Points or total fees you agreed to, call your loan officer and let them know that they either have to adjust their fees, or you will go elsewhere for your loan. This is a red flag, and you must ask yourself, "If they can't be honest at the beginning of the process, can they keep their word by the time signing takes place?"

Rule #30

"If the rate goes up or fees increase, refuse to continue with the loan."

There are four problems you will face, if you decide to find a new lender or broker:

> ➢ If you are purchasing a home, you have probably deposited earnest money in escrow; and if your loan doesn't fund on time that money can be held up in escrow by the seller. Remember, the funds may be

held in trust, jointly by both the buyer and the seller depending upon your purchase agreement.

> If rates have increased since you locked your loan, you will have to accept the higher interest rate (check the current par rate at www. mortgage-maze.net) if you go to another lender or broker. If they have gone down, you can benefit from a new loan.

> You may have to pay for another appraisal, if the current lender or broker won't release it.

> You must be willing to lose the house if you are purchasing a home.

If you can find a new lender and get the process done quickly, no harm, no foul. But the seller can always choose to cancel the purchase contract if you do not complete the loan within the stated contractual term. When refinancing, the rate increase and a possible new appraisal fee are the only dangers involved in refusing to accept the terms of your loan. You are under no obligation to complete your loan with a dishonest loan officer, and the only way the industry will change is if borrowers hold them accountable for their promises.

Conclusion

I believe the information contained is this guide will assist you in avoiding dishonest loan officers and the companies that employ them. Follow the suggestions in Chapter 8 and you will pin down the rate and fees associated with your loan. Don't accept any excuses on the part of the loan officer. If they are honest, there should be no problem making and keeping the commitments.

The vast majority of homeowners and buyers don't have any idea how the mortgage industry conducts itself. Now you do, and you can put your knowledge to work for you. It is high time that mortgage lenders and brokers know it is the borrower who must be happy with their loan, not them. Loan officers don't have to receive a year's wages on your loan. If they conduct themselves in an honest manner, they will have plenty of referrals.

An "A" paper borrower should never have to pay more than 1.5 Points for your loan. Sub-prime borrowers should not pay more than 2 Points for their loan. The time spent working on your loan is considerable, but there is no reason to pay over $5,000 to a lender or broker, no matter how large the loan, so insist on a cap to the broker or lender fees.

The lending industry will not change its ways without borrowers demanding that predatory lending practices and other outrageous actions cease. It's up to borrowers to change the way the mortgage industry conducts itself. When borrowers allow brokers and lenders to disregard their promises, it only invites further abuses.

Refuse to work with any loan officer who won't tell you what the total cost of your loan is, before you get started. If the loan officer isn't happy with any of the commitments you request, keep searching for one until you find an honest broker or lender. There are plenty of honest loan officers out there and now you have the tools to find them. Slick talk won't save you any money; straight answers will.

It is my hope that the industry can clean up its poor reputation. Together we can make this a reality.

"SUCCESSFULLY NAVIGATING THE MORTGAGE MAZE" MORTGAGE REVIEW SERVICE

Alan Jablonski, author of **"SUCCESSFULLY NAVIGATING THE MORTGAGE MAZE,"** understands how difficult it is for borrowers to read their loan documents to ensure they are getting the loan they were promised.

Although his book **"SUCCESSFULLY NAVIGATING THE MORTGAGE MAZE"** shows you how to read your loan documents, not all borrowers have the time to thoroughly review and understand their interest rate, APR, hidden fees, cost of their loan and whether there is a prepayment penalty associated with the loan.

For those people, Alan Jablonski has launched a mortgage review service that will give you the exact cost and terms of your loan. Alan will review your critical loan documents and provide you with an easy to read comprehensive review of your loan costs.

In an easy 3-step process all you do is:

1. Request these loan documents be e-mailed to you from your escrow agent:
    *   Truth in Lending Statement
    *   Estimated HUD-1
    *   Note

2. Visit our website at www.mortgage-maze.net and click on the "Review Documents" service and follow the simple instructions.

3. Within 48 hours we will return a complete review of your loan that tells you:
    *   Your *"real"* interest rate;
    *   The *"total"* cost of your loan (this includes up-front fees and any hidden fees that are included in your APR);
    *   If you have a prepayment penalty, if so, how long is the period;
    *   Do you have a hard or soft prepayment penalty?

It is in simple, easy to understand language, so anyone will understand the exact cost of their loan. You will know if your lender or broker gave the interest rate and fees the loan officer promised.

Peace of mind is hard to come by when a borrower is in the middle of the mortgage process. A second set of eyes is a great way to give you the information you need to either move forward with your loan or catch an unscrupulous loan officer in the lies that so many tell.

"SUCESSFULLY NAVIGATING THE MORTGAGE MAZE" SEMINARS

"What is an APR?"…. "How binding is a Good Faith Estimate?"…"Why isn't an Adjustable Rate Mortgage Right for me?"

These and other *"must know"* topics for the potential home buyer are addressed in Alan Jablonski's **"Successfully Navigating the Mortgage Maze"** seminars.

In a highly interactive format, Alan arms his audience with all the knowledge, strategies and tactics they need to protect themselves from predatory lenders and mortgage brokers, as well as providing them with step-by-step instructions on how to take control of the mortgage process. Alan explores in depth how to:

➤ Spot lies in the initial conversation

➤ Negotiate a better rate and fee structure

➤ Avoid pre-payment penalties

➤ Find the best rates available on any given day

➤ Understanding all the factors that determine your rate

➤ Find out if you are being charged hidden fees

"Successfully Navigating the Mortgage Maze" has been well-received by audiences ranging from police departments, colleges, public and non–profit companies. "Officers of the Los Angeles Airport Police came away from Alan's seminar understanding the importance of accurate credit reporting, how fraudulent reporting can have severe affects on their ability to maintain good credit scores, the mortgage process, how to decipher the baffling mortgage terminology, and how they could take control of the lending process" remarked Robert Rios, a Commander with the department.

Tailored to your particular audience, **"Successfully Navigating the Mortgage Maze"** can be customized to run from 1-3 hours. Members of the audience will also receive a complimentary copy of Alan Jablonski's **"Successfully Navigating the Mortgage Maze"** book along with a discount on his mortgage review service. For more information, Alan can be contacted at www.mortgage-maze.net.

Preferred Real Estate Services-A California Mortgage Broker

"Offering 1-Point California Loans"

Alan Jablonski, is a broker at Preferred Real Estate Services, and the author of the recently published, **SUCCESSFULLY NAVIGATING THE MORTGAGE MAZE**. He is also a much sought-after consumer rights presenter on mortgage issues.

To promote the launch of his home loan borrower's guide, Alan is offering any California resident that has purchased **SUCCESSFULLY NAVIGATING THE MORTGAGE MAZE** or attended one of his seminars a flat 1 Point fee for their loan. This includes up-front and rebate fees combined not including title, escrow and lender fees.

You will be amazed at how little a loan can cost!

Alan is California licensed mortgage broker based in Long Beach, California. He takes pride in the fact that he has a one-hundred percent funding record. None of his clients have ever defaulted on their loans because he won't fund a loan if the client can't afford the payments.

Alan stands behind the commitments that he suggests to his readers in **SUCCESSFULLY NAVIGATING THE MORTGAGE MAZE**. His clients not only have no surprises, but he won't recommend a loan unless there is a financial benefit to his clients.

> *"We were stuck in an Option ARM mortgage, facing ballooning monthly payments. Alan worked diligently with us…now we have a low rate fixed loan that is saving us hundreds of dollars a month…He does what he says he will do, and explains everything."*
>
> Cameron Kenady, borrower

You can visit Alan Jablonski's website at www.califlending.com for more information about your mortgage needs.

978-0-595-52145-6
0-595-52145-2

www.ingramcontent.com/pod-product-compliance
Lightning Source LLC
Chambersburg PA
CBHW030819180526
45163CB00003B/1354